UNDERSTANDING
AGATHA CHRISTIE

Agatha Christie

Tison Pugh

THE UNIVERSITY OF
SOUTH CAROLINA PRESS

© 2023 University of South Carolina

Published by the University of South Carolina Press
Columbia, South Carolina 29208

uscpress.com

Manufactured in the United States of America

32 31 30 29 28 27 26 25 24 23
10 9 8 7 6 5 4 3 2 1

Library of Congress Cataloging-in-Publication Data
can be found at http://catalog.loc.gov/.

ISBN 978-1-64336-440-7 (hardcover)
ISBN 978-1-64336-441-4 (paperback)
ISBN 978-1-64336-442-1 (ebook)

Portions of chapter 8 were previously published as "Queering Dame Agatha Christie: Barry Sandler's Camp Adaptation of *The Mirror Crack'd* (1980)," in *Queer/Adaptation: A Collection of Critical Essays,* edited by Pamela Demory (Palgrave Macmillan, 2019, 33–47).

In memory of my grandmothers:

Vivian Alexander Pugh,

whose freezer was always well stocked with ice-cream sandwiches,

and Camilla Tison Rachal,

who read the solutions of Agatha Christie's and other mysteries first and
then backtracked through the stories.

CONTENTS

The volumes of Understanding Contemporary British Literature (UCBL) have been planned as guides or companions for students as well as good nonacademic readers. The editor and publisher perceive a need for these volumes because much of the influential contemporary literature makes special demands. Uninitiated readers encounter difficulty in approaching works that depart from the traditional forms and techniques of prose and poetry. Literature relies on conventions, but the conventions keep evolving; new writers form their own conventions—which in time may become familiar. Put simply, UCBL provides instruction in how to read certain contemporary writers—identifying and explicating their material, themes, use of language, point of view, structures, symbolism, and responses to experience.

The word *understanding* in the titles was deliberately chosen. Many willing readers lack an adequate understanding of how contemporary literature works; that is, what the author is attempting to express and the means by which it is conveyed. Although the criticism and analysis in the series have been aimed at a level of general accessibility, these introductory volumes are meant to be applied in conjunction with the works they cover. They do not provide a substitute for the works and authors they introduce, but rather prepare the reader for more profitable literary experiences.

M.J.B.

THE MYSTERY OF AGATHA CHRISTIE'S TITLES

Many of Agatha Christie's novels were originally published under two titles, one for British and the other for American audiences—an issue briefly addressed on p. 42 of this volume. In writing and researching this book, I relied on *The Agatha Christie Mystery Collection*, an edition published by Bantam in the 1980s and 1990s. This series employs the American titles of Christie's books, and I have, for the most part, used these titles in the ensuing volume, despite that the Christie Estate has since standardized her titles to their original British publications. Any questions about the identity of a particular text mentioned in *Understanding Agatha Christie* can be resolved by consulting the bibliography, which includes all titles and their variants. The mystery remains, however, why anyone would pick *4:50 from Paddington* as a preferable title to *What Mrs. McGillicuddy Saw!*—even if it were Agatha herself—or why someone once insisted that *Death in the Clouds* should be retitled *Death in the Air*, surely a distinction without much of a difference.

ONE

Understanding Agatha Christie

The Seven Paradoxes of Her Appeal

I began this book approximately six months into the COVID-19 pandemic of 2020 because, like so many others secluded during the various states of lockdown, quarantine, and social isolation, I was bored. Remembering the speed, delight, and near-addictive obsession with which I tore through Agatha Christie's novels during my junior high school years, it occurred to me that they might provide a similarly pleasureful diversion almost four decades later. Midway through those forty years, I earned a PhD in English literature, and I have spent the last twenty years as an English professor teaching and researching medieval masterpieces, primarily the works of Geoffrey Chaucer and the Arthurian legends. Part of my education included the distinction between literary fiction (lauded as the masterworks of the field) and genre fiction (denigrated as potboilers and pulp fiction), and as English departments still lean decidedly toward the former, I wondered if Christie's murder mysteries, the genre fiction I voraciously consumed as a tweenager, would still pique my interest, appreciation, and admiration today. The short answer is: of course they did.

The remaining pages of this book divulge the longer answer to the question of Agatha Christie's legacy, in which I hypothesize seven paradoxical reasons for the extraordinary popularity of her fiction. More than one hundred years after the publication of her first novel, *The Mysterious Affair of Styles,* in 1920, and almost fifty years following her death in 1976, her popularity shows little sign of dimming. Certainly, she is deservedly celebrated for creating several masterworks of detective fiction, notably *The Murder of Roger Ackroyd, Murder on the Orient Express, The ABC Murders, Death on the Nile, And Then There Were None,* and *The Witness for the Prosecution,* along with a remarkably strong second-tier of novels, the names of which are not as widely known by the public but which amply reward readers exploring her canon more widely, including *Appointment with Death, The Moving Finger, The Hollow, Crooked House, The Pale Horse,* and *Endless Night.* Many of even the most devoted followers of Christie's canon admit their disappointment with some titles—frequent nominees in this category include *The Big Four, Passenger to Frankfurt,* and *Postern of Fate*—a circumstance rendered less surprising given the fact that Christie herself conceded her disappointment with some of her fiction, evident in her distaste for *The Mystery of the Blue Train:* "I have always hated *The Mystery of the Blue Train,* but I got it written, and sent [it] off to the publishers. It sold just as well as my last book had done."[1] With an output of more than eighty novels and short-story collections—some absolute gems, some sparkling a bit less brightly—the unevenness of Christie's output is hardly surprising. Such unevenness is true of every prolific author, including such foundational figures of British literature as Geoffrey Chaucer and William Shakespeare, yet Chaucer's *Tale of Melibee* and *Prioress's Tale,* generally acknowledged among the clunkers of the *Canterbury Tales,* and Shakespeare's *Pericles* and *Two Gentlemen of Verona* do not markedly detract from their authors' reputations as literary geniuses.

In contrast to Chaucer and Shakespeare, whose literary reputations stand as ensured as can be imagined, Christie has continually been derided as singularly untalented, despite her unassailable pride of place in popular culture. Some of the more withering criticisms directed her way arose from fellow mystery writers who denigrated her style, plotting, and productivity. Raymond Chandler opined that the solutions of her mysteries were "guaranteed to knock the keenest mind for a loop. Only a half-wit could guess it."[2] P. D. James, author of the Adam Dalgliesh mysteries, condemned her style as "neither original nor elegant but . . . workmanlike" and damned her with faint praise: "Perhaps her greatest strength was that she never overstepped the limits of her talent."[3] Vladimir Nabokov is rarely critically shoehorned as a mystery writer, yet his *Lolita* is littered with clues about the precise nature of Lolita's disappearance and the identity of the mysterious Clare Quilty; rather than discerning kinship with his fellow mystery author, Nabokov stated succinctly, "Agatha is unreadable."[4] Ruth Rendell, author of the Inspector Wexford series, averred that when holding one of Christie's novels, "I don't feel as though I have a piece of fiction worthy of the name in front of me."[5] Many of Christie's colleagues, past and present, dismissed her abilities, despite her overwhelming success in winning the attention of readers.

Many such criticisms of Christie's fiction overlook the necessity—or at least the pleasure—of a well-crafted puzzle structuring the plot of a murder mystery, and throughout the history of her critical reception, several reviewers have bluntly asserted that Christie could not write well while conceding her abilities as a puzzle fabricator. This line of thought is evident in Julian Symons's appraisal: "She was not a good writer," he asserts, although he acknowledges that "she was supreme mistress in the construction of puzzles and had a skill in writing light, lively and readable dialogue that has been consistently underrated by critics."[6] Michael Moon similarly views her popularity as resulting from "her exceptional ingenuity as a plotter and the reliable delivery of suspense and surprise in her narratives, combined with her straightforward ability as a storyteller and a scene-setter."[7] David Grossvogel dismisses her fiction as "never more than nostalgia and illusion" and proposes that "her continued success suggests only that the illusion has not yet receded completely beyond our ken."[8] Further to these points, some readers prefer Christie's peers to Christie and offer apples-and-oranges comparisons, as in Catherine Kenney's evident preference for Dorothy Sayers and her assessment that "Sayers was working in a genuinely novelistic tradition, while Christie used narrative simply as a way of structuring the detective puzzle," in which the adverbs *genuinely* and *simply,* as well the implied contrast between novels and puzzles, debase Christie's accomplishments.[9] As this brief overview of Christie's detractors indicates, many critics would delight in plunging a dagger through the metaphoric hearts of her novels, dispatching them so that future generations would be freed from her conspicuous faults.

Tellingly, however, Christie's novels often received rather glowing reviews from contemporary critics who assessed her achievements within the field of detective fiction and its expected parameters. The *New York Times* reviewer of *The ABC Murders* hailed it as "a baffler of the first water, written in Agatha Christie's best manner,"[10] and the *Time* reviewer praised *Death on the Nile* as "a story that is readable, implausible, but contains the most genuinely surprising solution of the month."[11] In a somewhat skeptical review of *Appointment with Death,* Kay Irvin nonetheless praised the author's corpus as a whole: "Even a lesser Agatha Christie story holds its readers' attention with its skillful management of suspense."[12] Paul Neimark's rave review of *Endless Night*—"Mrs. Christie has thrown down the gauntlet as never before and produced a surpassing mystery that is almost as fine a novel"—concluded by comparing her favorably to Thornton Wilder and Henry James.[13] Similarly comparing Christie to a stratospheric literary talent, J. C. Trewin wrote in a review of her play *Towards Zero:* "One thing is plain: though Shakespeare could have enriched the dialogue of Mrs. Christie's piece, she could have told him how to animate the plot of *Timon* [*of Athens*]."[14] What these critics see—and what so many others miss—is that Christie's work should be assessed according to the parameters of her métier of detective fiction, not to the nebulous aesthetic expectations of literary fiction. Robert Barnard summarized the views of Christie's myopic critics and their perpetual failure to convince readers not to read her works: "In fact, all the common grounds of criticism and ridicule used against Agatha Christie work with a boomerang effect when we realize that she was essentially, and aimed to be, a popular writer, a good teller of tales."[15]

Given these confused and confusing conditions between her unassailable and enduring popularity and the consistent drubbing meted out by many critics, readers (including her second husband, Max Mallowan) have posed the question of her appeal and posited their answers. Mallowan asked rhetorically, "What is it that has made for [her] overwhelming success?" and then theorized: "First the supreme art of telling a story, held by a continuous thread so that when you have read one chapter you cannot resist going on to the next."[16] Gillian Gill similarly queried, "Why is it that Agatha Christie is so phenomenally popular?" and volunteered that "Many other Golden Age novelists offered equally good puzzles . . . [but] Christie's unique contribution was to create an original fictional world that is both totally convincing and highly unrealistic."[17] John Cawelti identified the secret behind Christie's success as her "ability to design an unusually complex and well-balanced detection-mystification structure and to set it forth with enough character and atmosphere to give it some flesh but not enough to distract from the chain of inquiry that has made her the most successful living writer of the classical detective formula."[18] These theories and others of their ilk identify the appeal of Christie's novels in their rapid pacing and their puzzling plotting, as well as in their immersive quality that invites readers to lose themselves in these fictional worlds

Building on such foundational insights, *Understanding Agatha Christie* offers a sustained contribution to this longstanding discussion by theorizing seven paradoxical reasons behind Christie's phenomenal and long-lasting success. The next chapter, "Agatha Christie's Life and Puzzling Persona," offers a succinct biography of her life and times, including her childhood years in Torquay, her marriage to and divorce from Archie Christie, her subsequent marriage to Max Mallowan, and her growing success as the best-selling author of the century. More so, it posits that, whether purposefully or not, Christie cultivated an enigmatic image of herself over her decades in the public eye, notably owing to her mysterious eleven-day disappearance in 1926 but also to her steady refusal to publicize herself and her novels. Despite the tut-tutting of literary critics who proscribe reading fiction for the insights it provides into an author's life, Christie encodes various personal experiences into her novels, thereby rewarding readers who treat her life as somewhat of a mystery in itself.

Moving from the author to her fictions, the subsequent five chapters posit that Christie's popularity stems from the ways in which her novels upend ostensible binaries rooted in the creation and reception of mystery novels and thus fracture their generic expectations. "The Scofflaw of the Golden Age of Detective Fiction," this volume's third chapter, examines this celebrated period of literary production, usually dated between 1920 and 1940, in which the protocols of crime novels were increasingly, if only quasi officially, codified, and for which Christie showed little concern. Notably, many of the authors advocating inviolate precepts for mystery fiction were men, and Christie's defiance of their rules for fiction infuses a gendered resistance to many of her novels. With such works as *The Murder of Roger Ackroyd, The Mysterious Mr. Quin, A Murder Is Announced,* and *Endless Night,* Christie demonstrated the futility of constraining the genre's possibilities and expanded it to include features that her contemporaries condemned.

The next chapter, "The Hardboiled Queen of the Cozies," explores the tension between the subgenres of mystery fiction labeled *cozy* and *hardboiled.* Often lauded as the "Queen of the Cozies," Christie is widely lionized for her role in establishing the expected tropes of this gentler mode of detective fiction, yet this title obfuscates her deeper concerns with themes of violence and its repercussions. Furthermore, the generic binary of *cozy* and *hardboiled* establishes an unnecessary gendered division—as the vast majority of gendered divisions are—between male and female authors of crime novels, as well as between their readers. This gendered division is further evident in the fact that several male authors of hardboiled fiction are increasingly enjoying recognition for their talents as literary authors, in another (wearying) instance of the denigration directed at artistic works associated too strongly with women's talents and tastes. Given these conditions, it is apparent that the somewhat arbitrary designation of Christie as a writer of cozy fiction, whether purposefully or unintentionally, undercuts an objective view of women's writing, with clearly pejorative repercussions to her authorial reputation.

Although many critics, including those cited a few pages earlier, dismissed Christie as a singularly bad writer, the following chapter, "The Poet of Genre Fiction," takes seriously her poetic efforts—evident in the fact that she published several poems prior to *The Mysterious Affair at Styles* and continued writing verse throughout her life. Critics have also derided her poems as singularly dreadful, but the very fact that she pursued poetry alongside her prose publications highlights her interest in the aesthetic beauty of language across genres. Furthermore, many critics of Christie's fiction appear strikingly unaware of the unique rhetorical and structural demands that mystery novels place on their authors, and this chapter also outlines her awareness of the genre's requirements for settings, characters, and plots and her refusal to reframe them to the contours of literary fiction. Counterbalancing her predominant interest in murder mysteries and genre fiction, Christie's six novels penned under the pseudonym Mary Westmacott—*Giant's Bread* (1930), *Unfinished Portrait* (1934), *Absent in the Spring* (1944), *The Rose and the Yew Tree* (1948), *A Daughter's a Daughter* (1952), and *The Burden* (1956)—collectively demonstrate her fluency with the protocols of literary fiction. Briefly, both Christie's novels and her commentaries on fiction writing evince her awareness of the distinctions between genre and literary fiction, as well as her reasons for adhering to certain tropes of genre fiction and for refusing to adopt certain tropes of literary fiction.

Several of Christie's novels, despite their bloodied corpses and tense investigations, are as amusing as they are enigmatic, and the chapter "The Tragicomic Themes of Christie's Murders," examines her particular brand of humor as influenced by the comedy of manners tradition. A sardonic comic tone infuses many of Christie's novels as characters grapple with the social implications of murder, such as when one character wonders whether she will find herself the next victim and her interlocutor deadpans in reply: "Well, Edith . . . it depends so much, does it not, by whom the murder was committed?" (*Clocks*, 49). Interweaving complementary contrasts to such comic touches, Christie imbues many of her novels with tragic elements, which undercuts criticisms of the novels as insufficiently emotionally invested with their characters. Untimely deaths, even those of the miserable, the miserly, and the malicious, leave emptiness, confusion, and uncertainty about life's transience in their wake, and Christie often showcases the emotional repercussions of murder while untangling the threads cloaking the killer. The paradox of Christie's tragicomic themes expands the emotional impact of her tales, resulting in mysteries that might amuse, or sadden, or otherwise achieve a range of emotional reactions from readers beyond the intellectual satisfaction of her well-constructed puzzles.

The English settings of the vast majority of Christie's novels reflect a hidebound and musty world, one with very little concern given to the representations of minorities of race, ethnicity, gender, sexuality, physical ability, and other markers of personal identity. In short, Christie's characters inhabit a very white, rather wealthy, and fairly stuffy world. Yet at the same time that Christie naturalizes a white version of Englishness reflective of her upbringing and conservative worldview, she also embeds withering critiques of England and Englishness. This paradoxical tension is explored in the next chapter, "The Queer Insularity of Christie's England." Writing during and after the peak of British imperialism, Christie captures a world where many characters might prefer to revivify the "good old days" of England's international hegemony, yet they must simultaneously confront the ways in which odd and othered characters, including her primary detectives Hercule Poirot and Miss Jane Marple, resist facile and constraining constructions of Englishness. Upon closer examination, Christie's England appears to be a queer place, more than one might initially expect.

The final chapter, "Christie's Murders at the Movies . . . and Why She Disliked Them," identifies the importance of cinematic and theatrical adaptations of Christie's novels to her continuing success as a cultural icon. Christie regularly denounced these adaptations, lamenting the shifts in character and tone and lambasting particularly egregious, or simply creative, reimaginings of her works, but these adaptations have enlivened her source texts and maintained their vibrancy for subsequent generations. Following a necessarily brief overview of adaptations of Christie's works in film and television, the chapter examines in depth the 1980 adaptation of *The Mirror Crack'd,* penned by screenwriter Barry Sandler, who shares his insights about the value of camp humor for adapting Christie's mysteries. Christie praised relatively few productions of her novels, with the rare exceptions of Billy Wilder's *Witness for the Prosecution* (1957) and Sidney Lumet's *Murder on the Orient Express* (1974), but regardless of whether she would have enjoyed or disdained the film adaptation of *The Mirror Crack'd,* it exemplifies the manifold possibilities of reframing her mysteries in ways she likely never anticipated.

When today's literary critics attempt to demolish the reputations of contemporary writers of genre fiction, I am always tempted to caution them with the lessons of history, precisely because many works recognized today as literary classics are rooted in genre fiction. Early writers of science fiction, horror fiction, and mystery fiction are today respected as canonical authors worthy of critical praise and continued attention, including such names as H. G. Wells and Jules Verne; Mary Shelley and Bram Stoker; Edgar Allan Poe and Anna Katharine Green.[19] Their reputations rose and fell as the centuries passed, and it is probable that the same fate is awaiting Agatha Christie. In his poem "Agatha Christie and Beatrix Potter," John Updike praises Christie as "Full of cheerful art and nearly / Perfect craft."[20] Updike's poem brilliantly juxtaposes two authors often overlooked in discussions of literary greatness whose fiction will likely be read long past contemporary critical darlings. Perhaps, as discussed briefly in this volume's conclusion, "Literary Criticism and the Mystery of Christie's Murderous Pleasures," if literary criticism changed its focus from purportedly great works to those stories that provide the greatest lasting pleasure, it would better respect the reading public and better theorize the manifold joys of literature. In *Understanding Agatha Christie,* my goal is to explore the pleasures of Christie's texts, the scope of her achievements, and these seven paradoxes key to her lasting appeal, rather than to worry about any snobs who would not stain their hands with a book jacket featuring a bloodied corpse.

TWO

Agatha Christie's Life and Puzzling Persona

One need know nothing about an author to enjoy her novels. Literary pleasures arise from the words on the page, from the plot that unfolds, and from the characters that the author brings to life as readers advance from beginning to end. At the same time, readers often feel an ephemeral sense of connection, even kinship, with the authors whose fiction they particularly enjoy, and such a connection should not be discounted as an unsophisticated response. When readers profess that they "like" or "love" Geoffrey Chaucer or Zora Neale Hurston or Gabriel García Márquez, they likely mean that they enjoy these authors' writings, but the authors simultaneously become enmeshed with their literature—in effect, they transform into a metonymic representation of their own works. In discerning the interplay of authors' lives and of the literature that they have produced, some readers discover an engaging entryway into their texts, and, from this viewpoint, Agatha Christie's biography and public persona admit another venue for exploring the pleasure that so many readers have found in her mysteries. Within this paradoxical perspective, Christie's life story enhances an appreciation of her works, even as such information can be wholly overlooked when reading them.

Born 15 September 1890 in Torquay, a seaside town of Devon, England, Dame Agatha Mary Clarissa Miller Christie (who would later become Lady Mallowan) enjoyed an idyllic upbringing. "I had a very happy childhood" (3), she stated simply in her *Autobiography*, remembering her early years as the youngest child in her family of five, comprised of parents Frederick and Clara Miller, sister Margaret Frary ("Madge," born January 1879), and brother Louis Montant ("Monty," born June 1880).[1] Agatha claimed that "the first memory that springs up in my mind is a clear picture of myself walking along the streets of Dinard on market day with my mother" (*Autobiography*, xii), while also stating that it is "difficult to know what one's first memory is. I remember distinctly my third birthday" (*Autobiography*, 9). Despite the fog of recollecting one's youth, Agatha relished her childhood in the family home of Ashfield and was particularly fond of Tony, the family's Yorkshire terrier, reportedly named for George Washington (*Autobiography*, 21). Apparently, she did not overly object to Monty's nickname for her: the "scrawny chicken."

Agatha's parents, Frederick Alvah Miller, a wealthy New Yorker with business interests in England, and Clara Margaret Boehmer, married in 1878; they met through family connections, as Frederick was Clara's aunt's stepson. The newlywed Millers established their residence in Torquay when Clara purchased Ashfield. Agatha describes the family as modestly, not aristocratically, wealthy: "Actually, he [her father Frederick] was merely comfortably off. We did not have a butler or a footman. We did not have a carriage and horses and a coachman. We had three servants, which was a minimum then" (*Autobiography*, 33–34). Due to the mishandling of family funds and possible embezzlement, Frederick's income diminished over the years, leading the family to a variety of economizing strategies, including renting out Ashfield and living in France (Pau, Cauterets, Paris, and Brittany) in the late 1890s. (Although today one would hardly consider a lengthy stay in France as a cost-cutting measure, in those years wealthy English families could enjoy a profit from leasing their homes and then traveling on the continent.) During their French sojourn Clara hired Marie Sijé as Agatha's companion and French instructor. Certainly, Agatha's education could be described as mostly informal yet highly effective, as she recalled: "In those days . . . girls rarely went to school. Usually they had a nurse, and later, perhaps, a governess. As education, one had classes, piano classes, dancing and cookery classes." She notes further that her mother "had been persuaded that education was hard on a child's eyes and brain, so I was kept at home" (Petschek, "Agatha Christie," 129).

When Agatha was eleven, her father suffered a series of cardiac ailments; during his convalescence, she wrote to him, "Darling Daddy, I am so sorry you are still ill, we miss you very much" (Thompson. *Agatha Christie,* 33). Frederick died soon after, at the age of fifty-five, leaving his family in such pressing economic straits that Clara considered selling Ashfield. Financial pressures were partially alleviated when Madge married James Watts in 1902 and ascended to a life of great wealth, for Agatha's new brother-in-law was the heir to Abney Hall, in the northwest of England, near Manchester. During these years Madge appeared the more likely sister to achieve literary acclaim, as she published several short stories in *Vanity Fair.* Brother Monty, if not quite the black sheep of the family, struggled to establish himself in a career. Over the years he followed a range of pursuits, including enlisting in the second Boer War of 1899; traveling to India, Kenya, and Uganda; planning a business of cargo boats on Lake Victoria; enlisting again in World War I as part of the King's African Rifles; and then returning home to convalesce after being shot in the arm. Agatha summarized the outcome of these actions in a single sentence: "[Brother Monty] was, alas, unsatisfactory from the point of view of making a success of life" (*Autobiography*, 105).

In 1905 Clara journeyed with adolescent Agatha to Paris, where she resided for approximately two years while attending several schools (under such headmistresses as Mademoiselle T., Miss Hogg, and Miss Dryden) and pursuing her musical interests in voice and piano. At the age of sixty-three, Agatha replied to the question, "If not yourself, who would you be?" with the answer "an opera singer" (Thompson, *Agatha Christie*, 60), testifying to her enduring passion for the musical arts and her lasting regrets that her performance anxieties had derailed her ambitions in piano and that her singing voice lacked sufficient timbre and strength for her operatic ambitions. Contemporaneous with her musical pursuits, Agatha undertook some early attempts at writing, and she credited her interest in the literary arts to her mother's admonitions during a childhood sickness: "It was my mother who told me to write. . . . I was in bed with a bad cold, and she said: 'You'd better write a short story. . . . Nonsense, don't say you can't! Of course you can!'"[2] After her years in France, Agatha debuted socially in Egypt, a journey which in part inspired her first novel-length but unpublished effort, *Snow upon the Desert*. The stunningly prolific novelist Eden Phillpotts, a Devon resident and family friend, wrote to her to encourage her efforts: "Some of these things that you have written . . . are capital. You have a great feeling for dialogue. You should stick to gay natural dialogue. Try and cut all moralizations out of your novels; you're much too fond of them, and nothing is more boring to read" (*Autobiography*, 183). When her career was firmly established, Agatha dedicated *Peril at End House* to Phillpotts: "To whom I shall always be grateful for . . . the encouragement he gave me many years ago."

During and after her social debut in Egypt, Agatha's early forays in courtship testify to her charm and appeal. Several men proposed marriage to her (or to her through her mother), among them Captain Hibberd, Bolton Fletcher, Wilfred Pirie, and Reggie Lucy. Agatha met Archibald Christie, a second lieutenant in the Royal Field Artillery, in 1912. With the outbreak of World War I on 28 July 1914, their courtship faced challenging obstacles, and Clara expressed hesitations over Archie, particularly owing to his relative indigence. The young couple did not waver in their affections and married on Christmas Eve of 1914. Archie soon joined the Royal Flying Corps, pursuing a career as a pilot, and as her contribution to the war effort, Agatha served in a hospital dispensary as part of the Voluntary Aid Detachment.

So impressed by the medicines and poisons surrounding her, Agatha wrote a poem titled "In a Dispensary": "Here is sleep and solace and soothing of pain— courage and vigour new! / Here is menace and murder and sudden death!—in these phials of green and blue!"[3] Although the literati might denounce such verse as doggerel, Agatha achieved notable success in her early pursuit of the poetic arts, publishing several poems in an array of venues. The decisive moment in Agatha's authorial career occurred when her sister Madge challenged her to write a mystery novel. Agatha recalled Madge's words—"I don't think you could do it . . . They are very difficult to do"—and Agatha's recalcitrant reaction will appeal to anyone whose intelligence and abilities were ever dismissed by an elder sibling: "From that moment on I was fired by the determination that I would write a detective story" (*Autobiography*, 198). And so she did: in 1916 Agatha began writing *The Mysterious Affair at Styles,* which featured the debut of one of fiction's most famous and enduring detectives, Hercule Poirot, as well as his sidekick, Captain Arthur Hastings.

During the late 1910s and into the mid-1920s, Agatha viewed writing more as an avocation than as a vocation, prioritizing her personal life over her nascent profession. She expressed her contentment with marriage and family life, and both Archie and Agatha appeared very much in love. In a letter dated 4 April 1917, Archie wrote to Agatha, "I do really love you. . . . No one else would be the same to me. Never desert me darling and always love me" (Thompson, *Agatha Christie*, 91). Following the end of World War I in 1918, Agatha devoted much of her energy to domestic life. Now four years into their marriage, the Christies began married life anew, cohabiting as husband and wife for the first time. The young family grew with the birth of Rosalind Margaret Clarissa Christie on 5 August 1919; Agatha memorably described pregnancy as "like a nine-month ocean voyage to which you never got acclimatized" (*Autobiography*, 253).

With *The Mysterious Affair at Styles* completed, Agatha suffered the indignities of rejection meted out to so many promising young authors, until finally submitting the manuscript to John Lane at the Bodley Head. After a seemingly interminable period waiting for a response, she was invited to revise the manuscript for further consideration. It was then accepted, and she signed a contract for five additional books. *The Secret Adversary* followed in 1922, and this book introduced Christie's recurring characters of Tommy and Tuppence Beresford (who were unmarried in the first installment of their adventures).

Archie took a new position as the financial advisor of the forthcoming 1924 Empire Exhibition, serving under the authority of his rather peculiar and demanding boss, Major Ernest R. Belcher, who inspired the enigmatic figure of Sir Eustace Pedler in Agatha's *The Man in the Brown Suit.* As part of the requirements of Archie's job, the Christies traveled the world throughout 1922, with stops in Cape Town, Johannesburg, and Pretoria in South Africa; Melbourne, Sydney, Queensland, and Tasmania in Australia; New Zealand; Fiji; Honolulu, Hawaii; Winnipeg, Banff, Toronto, and Ottawa in Canada; and New York City. During their days in Hawaii, Agatha learned to surf.

If sibling rivalry with Madge to some degree inspired *The Mysterious Affair at Styles,* perhaps sibling rivalry with Agatha, now a published novelist, inspired Madge to pen *The Claimant,* her play produced in London in 1924. *The Claimant* is loosely based on a notorious case of the 1860s and 1870s, in which Thomas Castro, an Australian butcher, declared himself the lost heir to the Tichborne baronetcy. Despite Madge's ambitions, Agatha was destined to be the premier, and certainly the more prolific, author of the family, evident in the fact that 1924 witnessed the publication of three works: her short-story collection *Poirot Investigates,* her adventure novel *The Man in the Brown Suit,* and her poetry collection *The Road of Dreams.* As evident from these and her other titles from the 1920s and early 1930s, Agatha was experimenting with a range of genres and literary forms at this point of her career, including light-hearted thrillers (e.g., *The Secret of Chimneys, The Seven Dials Mystery*) and her first novel published under the pseudonym Mary Westmacott, *Giant's Bread.*

Dissatisfied with her royalty rates and feeling as well that John Lane had taken advantage of her naiveté as a young author, Agatha left Bodley Head after *The Secret of Chimneys* for a new publishing house, Collins, where she found more generous terms; she also signed with the Hughes Massie literary agency. In 1926 Agatha's published her breakthrough novel, *The Murder of Roger Ackroyd,* with Collins. Her brother-in-law James Watts reportedly inspired this novel by proposing that the murderer of a mystery novel should be the Watson character—a suggestion also put forth by Lord Mountbatten (Mallowan, *Mallowan's Memoirs,* 208). With her increased funds she purchased a luxury item— a grey Morris Cowley car. Tending to family matters, Madge and Agatha bought a cottage in Dartmoor for Monty, and Agatha hired Charlotte Fisher, a longtime fixture in the family who worked as Rosalind's nanny and Agatha's typist.

Agatha's burgeoning success and apparently happy home life could not protect her from the traumas of 1926, a year marred by personal tragedies. Her mother Clara died on 5 April, and her marriage effectively ended when Archie confessed his romantic relationship with Nancy Neele and requested a divorce. "I've fallen in love with her, and I'd like you to give me a divorce as soon as it can be arranged" (*Autobiography,* 338), she recalls he said, as she recalled as well her resistance: "I stood out for a year, hoping he would change. But he did not" (340). The dissolution of her marriage prompted the still-mysterious circumstances of her eleven-day disappearance beginning 4 December 1926, when she vanished after abandoning her car (the Morris) at the edge of a quarry in Newlands Corner, near the village of Albury. Part of the oddness of this course of events is that it appears that she did not wish to vanish entirely: she also wrote a letter to her brother-in-law, Campbell Christie, informing him that she would be convalescing at a Yorkshire spa. Quite oddly, Agatha registered in this hotel under the name of Archie's mistress, Nancy Neele. Agatha's disappearance sparked international headlines, and Deputy Chief Constable Kenward of the Surrey Constabulary oversaw the search for her—or, as it was feared, for her body; nearby ponds were dragged as part of the investigation.

But was Agatha kidnapped, or murdered (maybe by Archie?), or did she disappear on her own volition, perhaps as part of the research for a new novel or simply as a publicity stunt? Some theorized that she was "disguised and probably in male attire" and would "be found living in London."[4] Or perhaps she staged her disappearance in a manner to frame Archie, thus to avenge herself for their incipient divorce and to render his marriage to Nancy Neele impossible? Such questions swirled around the nation during her disappearance, and as an investigative expert wrote in the *Daily Mail:* "One great difficulty is that the search is for a woman with certain attributes that are not so common to the ordinary individual. She is talented. She is a woman who by the very nature of her work would have an exceptionally elastic brain. Consequently, one would expect her, consciously or subconsciously, to do something extraordinary" (Thompson, *Agatha Christie,* 213). The case was solved not by the police but by Bob Tappin and Bob Leeming, two members of the band at the Harrogate Hydro (now known as The Old Swan Hotel), the spa where Agatha took refuge after abandoning her car. Tappin and Leeming informed the local police of the remarkable resemblance between Agatha Christie and the hotel's guest known as Mrs. Neele, and the mystery that gripped the nation was quickly solved.

Archie blamed the incident on amnesia—"She does not know who she is" (Thompson, *Agatha Christie,* 238)—and Dr. Donald Core of Manchester University and Dr. Henry Wilson, the Watts family physician, affirmed his assessment: "After a careful examination of Mrs. Agatha Christie this afternoon we have formed the opinion that she is suffering from an unquestionably genuine loss of memory, and that for her future welfare she should be spared all anxiety and excitement."[5] Amnesia erases Agatha of any responsibility for her disappearance, notwithstanding the inherent implausibility that a person could lose her memory and yet function perfectly normally. On the contrary, most people truly suffering from amnesia would alert others to their condition so that they could relearn their identities and regain their lost lives, and it is remarkably odd that, as an amnesiac, Agatha would forget her own name but remember and adopt that of her husband's mistress. Indeed, a *New York Times* article on these inscrutable events mentions that "a number of mental specialists in London are still inclined not to accept entirely the bulletin issued after Mrs. Christie's examination."[6] Whatever motivated Agatha's disappearance remains a mystery; she refused to talk publicly of these perplexing events of December 1926. The Christies' divorce was finalized in 1928, and Archie married Nancy Neele soon after, with their son, Rosalind's half-brother, born in 1930. Agatha freely admitted her heartbreak over Archie's betrayal: "I had married the man I loved, and we had a child, we had somewhere to live, and as far as I could see there was no reason why we shouldn't live happily ever after" (*Autobiography,* 262).

Following this tumultuous period, Agatha's career continued its inexorable ascent. Foremost, she acknowledged a noted shift in her status as an author, realizing that she would now write novels even when she preferred not to: "That was the moment when I changed from an amateur to a professional. I assumed the burden of a profession, which is to write even when you don't want to, don't much like what you're writing, and aren't writing particularly well" (*Autobiography,* 344). Planning a winter vacation in 1928 to the Caribbean, on a whim Agatha exchanged her tickets for a journey on the Orient Express to Istanbul, Damascus, and Baghdad, during which she met the famed archeologist Leonard Woolley and his wife Katharine. On a return trip to Ur, she was introduced to Max Edgar Lucien Mallowan, an archeologist fourteen years her junior. Agatha accompanied Max on an expedition to various ruins, during which their car became stuck in the sand. For Max, this moment catalyzed his attraction to his companion: "I remember being amazed that Agatha did not reproach me for my incompetence . . . and I then decided that she must be a remarkable woman" (Mallowan, *Mallowan's Memoirs,* 45). Upon learning that Rosalind had contracted pneumonia, Agatha returned to England, with Max accompanying her. In 1929 Agatha's brother Monty died from a stroke.

Agatha and Max married in 1930, which marked a new beginning of her personal life. In subsequent years she joined him on numerous excursions to the Middle East, where she assisted in his excavations by photographing and cataloging artifacts while also finding time to write her novels. During the years 1933 to 1938 she wintered in Iraq and Syria on Mallowan's excavations and summered in Torquay. Alongside these events, the 1930s marked a period of astounding productivity. In 1930 she introduced the second of her most famous detectives, Miss Jane Marple, in this character's first novel, *The Murder at the Vicarage,* and she also enjoyed her first noted theatrical success: the production of her play, *Black Coffee,* which opened at the Embassy Theatre in London on 8 December. In 1934 alone, she published five books—*The Listerdale Mystery, Why Didn't They Ask Evans?, Parker Pyne Investigates, Murder in Three Acts,* and one of her foremost classics, *Murder on the Orient Express.* Agatha's experiences on Max's archeological excavations influenced a range of novels, notably in the period between 1936 and 1938, which saw the publication of *Murder in Mesopotamia, Death on the Nile,* and *Appointment with Death,* all of which are set in the Middle East. In the same year, Agatha published her second novel under the "Mary Westmacott" pseudonym: *Unfinished Portrait,* a semi-autobiographical novel detailing the breakup of a marriage that mirrors her failing relationship with Archie. She closed this decade with *And Then There Were None,* another of her masterpieces, and one of which she was particularly proud: "I don't say [*And*

Then There Were None] is my best, but I do think in some ways that is a better piece of *craftsmanship* than anything else I have written" (*Autobiography*, 458).[7]

World War II overshadowed the life of virtually all Europeans during the 1940s, but the war years did not slow down Agatha's amazing productivity, including such noted works as *Murder in Retrospect* (1942), *The Moving Finger* (1942), *The Hollow* (1946), *Witness for the Prosecution* (1948), and *Crooked House* (1949), along with theatrical adaptations of *And Then There Were None, Death on the Nile* (as *Hidden Horizon*), *Appointment with Death,* and *Towards Zero.* Under her Mary Westmacott pseudonym, she published *Absent in the Spring* in 1944, a riveting character study of a woman confronting her shallow vision of her life, her family, and herself. Such a colossal output becomes even more eyebrow-raising when one realizes that Agatha also penned Hercule Poirot's and Miss Marple's final mysteries, *Curtain* and *Sleeping Murder,* during this period, to be published if she died during a London bombing.

As she did during World War I, Agatha supported the war effort by volunteering at the dispensary of University College Hospital, and Max worked with the Anglo-Turkish Relief Committee and the Directorate of Allied and Foreign Liaison, and as a squadron leader in Cairo. One of the Mallowans' homes, Greenway, was requisitioned for war use by American officers. World War II, as Gill Plain argues, also influenced the contours of Christie's fiction, as the novels of this period "register the effects of trauma and social change" owing to their status as "product[s] of 'war climate.'"[8]

While allowing for the maxim that the only two people who truly know the state of a marriage are the couple themselves, the Mallowans' marriage appeared a companionable and affectionate one. Max wrote to Agatha in a letter dated 22 December 1943: "What I treasure in you is your imagination, that has been a continual stimulus to me, needful to the scholarly side, our love and affection without which life is a drab thing, your enthusiasm, freshness and vitality, your capacity for sharing my interests and enjoyments" (Thompson, *Agatha Christie,* 326). Somewhere along the way the Mallowans coined pet names for each other, and as the case with many such endearments, they are both intriguing yet cloying: Mr. and Mrs. Puper. Despite Agatha's impressive successes and eye-popping royalty checks, during this era she was plagued by financial headaches and hassles, notably owing to the efforts of the United States to tax her US profits, a situation that was further complicated by British efforts to tax her overseas profits.

Some of Agatha's readers mark the 1950s as the beginning of her decline, with her novels becoming more formulaic, offering fewer surprises, and occasionally echoing older plots. Such an assessment fails to take into account that, notwithstanding the constraints of genre fiction and her own productivity, Agatha created several daring works during this decade: the jaunty spy thriller *They*

Came to Baghdad (1951), her meditations on the meaning of family in *Ordeal by Innocence* (1958), and her keen portrayals of women's labor in *What Mrs. McGillicuddy Saw!* (1957) and *Cat among the Pigeons* (1959). As Agatha was by this time well-established as publishing at least one book a year, she nearly achieved a similar feat by staging so many plays in the 1950s: *The Hollow, The Mousetrap, Witness for the Prosecution, Spider's Web, Verdict,* and *The Unexpected Guest.* More so, any dismissive view of her accomplishments in the 1950s overlooks her greatest theatrical success: the opening of *The Mousetrap* on 5 November 1952, at the Ambassadors Theatre, which would become the longest running play in the history of Western drama, only shutting down in 2020 owing to the COVID-19 pandemic. Agatha originally wrote *The Mousetrap*, first titled *Three Blind Mice*, as a radio sketch on the occasion of Queen Mary's Eightieth Birthday Festival Programme.

As some literary critics overlook Agatha's novelistic achievements, so too do many theatre critics overlook her contributions to the history of the twentieth-century stage, yet as Julius Green documents, Agatha is "the most successful female playwright of all time." In addition to the incomparable run of *The Mousetrap,* she is, as Green asserts, "the only female playwright to have had three of her works running in the West End simultaneously."[9] Agatha enjoyed another theatrical success with *Witness for the Prosecution,* which opened in 1953; she declared it "the best play I have written."[10] In 1954 the Mystery Writers of America selected her for their inaugural Grand Master of Crime Award, and in 1956 she was honored with the Order of the British Empire. Her confrontations with tax authorities continued, necessitating creative financial arrangements, including donating royalties from books to charities and the founding of Agatha Christie Limited, a business that paid her a salary. Agatha gave the royalties from *The Mousetrap* to her grandson Mathew Prichard, who was born in 1943 and whose father was killed soon after in the invasion of Normandy. At the time, neither she nor the boy recognized the full extent of her generosity. Agatha's remarkable productivity continued in the 1960s, which witnessed the release of additional daring and creative works, particularly *The Pale Horse* (1961), *A Caribbean Mystery* (1964), and *Endless Night* (1967). In 1966 she published *Third Girl,* generally considered one of her lesser works, but the Mallowans celebrated another publication this year with Max's two-volume *Nimrud and Its Remains,* his magnum opus. As the years passed and Agatha's fame grew, so did Max's, although in the much more circumscribed realm of Middle Eastern archeology. He served as director of the British School of Archaeology in Iraq and as Professor of Western Asiatic Archaeology at the London University Institute of Archaeology. Agatha's grandson Mathew married in 1967. Agatha's and Max's health deteriorated at first slightly but then more noticeably: hers from psoriasis and his from a series of minor strokes. Agatha's last trip to the Middle East was in 1967.

In 1971 Agatha was named Dame Commander, Order of the British Empire. Many of even her most devoted readers concede that her powers were dimming in the 1970s, as she entered her eighties. *Nemesis* (1971) stands as the strongest of this period, featuring Miss Marple solving a mystery bequeathed to her by a deceased acquaintance, Jason Rafiel, with whom she allied herself during the events of *A Caribbean Mystery.* Agatha's last novel, *Postern of Fate* (1973), depicts the final appearance of Tommy and Tuppence Beresford, and although they charm as always with their affection, common sense, and derring-do, the mystery they solve is badly disjointed and lacks the satisfying solution of so many of her finer works. Critics decried her later works as subpar efforts—in Ralph Tyler's misogynistic view, they represented "the nattering of an inattentive woman over her yarn."[11] Linguistic analyses of Agatha's fiction indicate the likely cause of this decline as early-stage Alzheimer's disease. As Anne Kingston documents, *Elephants Can Remember* (1972), Agatha's penultimate novel, "contained a thirty percent drop in vocabulary compared to her writing at age sixty-three, eighteen percent more repeated phrases, and a nearly threefold increase in indefinite nouns"—all signs of a writer struggling to find her words.[12] A retrospective short-story collection, *Poirot's Early Cases,* was published in 1974, and her prewritten final novels for Hercule Poirot and Miss Marple were published afterward: *Curtain* in 1975, *Sleeping Murder* in 1976. Agatha broke her hip in 1971, and in October 1974 suffered a heart attack; she died on 12 January 1976, in Berkshire, Wallingford, and was buried at St. Mary's Church, Cholsey. Her headstone reads, "Sleep after toyle, port after stormie seas, / Ease after war, death after life does greatly please," a quotation from Edmund Spenser's *Faerie Queen.*[13] Max married Barbara Hastings Parker, a fellow archeologist, but died soon after, in August 1978.

As this chapter records the events of Agatha Christie's life, it can only hint at the enigmas of her personality and her family relationships, which continue to intrigue readers in the interplay between fact and fiction. Notwithstanding her life in the public eye for nearly six decades, Agatha refused much of the attention directed toward her. Indeed, Margaret Mochrie, observing in a 1937 article that Agatha refused nearly all interview requests, dubbed her "the Greta Garbo of mystery-story writers."[14] But also like the reclusive Garbo, Agatha paradoxically amplified her fame and appeal despite her distaste for the limelight, and so it matters little whether she purposefully molded her public persona or whether it accurately reflects her interior desires and identity. With the rise of the Hollywood star system and the increasing visibility of public figures across media platforms throughout the twentieth century, many celebrities such as Agatha

Christie developed public personas in a manner similar to film stars, whether they desired to do so or not, even if they were not devised as publicity campaigns by movie studios or publishing houses.

As Richard Dyer writes in his foundational study of stardom, "Stars are like characters in stories, representations of people."[15] In a circular process, fans begin to admire a celebrity and thus develop expectations about appropriate roles for this star, which the star and studio system capitalize on to increase the star's media presence and the financial payoffs of related projects. Further explicating the cultural work of stars and celebrity personas, Sean Redmond comments, "Stars and celebrities are often supericonic figures, who embody model identity positions that speak to certain psychic, cultural and economic needs."[16] Authors inhabit a distinct yet related type of stardom than movie stars, yet it is apparent that several twentieth-century authors, such as Truman Capote, Ernest Hemingway, James Baldwin, and Dorothy Parker, paid attention to the public's reception of their works and their selves. At the very least, as Agatha's fame as an author increased, so did interest in the person/persona of "Agatha" as mediated through her limited press appearances, and as her name became inseparable from her novels, her life became another lens through which to interpret her fictions. Certainly, Christie's grandson, Mathew Prichard, recognized her as a star, mentioning "the period in my childhood when I spent the most time with her, and became aware what a *star* she was (even though she hated people saying that!),"[17] even as he also acknowledged that "she hated being famous."[18] And so whether readers and fans recognized her as a real person—Agatha Christie—or as a person who constructed her public image through her refusal to do so—that is, "Agatha Christie"—the outward persona of "Agatha Christie" contrasted with the truth of her life.

Foremost, "Agatha Christie" is defined by her Englishness, as she is counted among the quintessential customs, artifacts, and citizens—Big Ben and high tea, King Arthur and Jane Austen, Stonehenge and steam trains—that define the English character within the world's popular imaginary. In complementary readings, Andrew Norman suggests that Agatha "loved so much of what, in her time, was regarded as being quintessentially English,"[19] and Christopher Yiannitsaros suggests that she herself became an emblem of "quintessential Englishness": "As one of England's most popular literary exports, Agatha's fictional works have become synonymous with ideas of what it might mean to be 'English,' while the author herself has been imaginatively transfigured into a battalion of English national identity."[20] Certainly, such a presumption should at least provoke a raised eyebrow, for if Agatha Christie herself is viewed as one of the defining symbols of Englishness, would not murder, along with roses, Westminster Abbey, and Queen Elizabeth II's corgis, represent the nation's character as well? More so, to view her as somehow transcendentally English overlooks her father's American roots and thus again points to the ways in which she bridges disparate cultural traditions. These quibbles aside, Agatha Christie's Englishness captures an ephemeral yet compelling part of her allure (an issue that is addressed in greater detail in chapter 7).

In the rare interviews that Agatha granted, she presented herself as a retiring figure, one who avoided the limelight and lived quietly among her family and friends. In a self-deprecating assessment, she declared: "I'm a moderately intelligent, moderately industrious and quite simple woman, who has been remarkably lucky."[21] She abstained from alcohol and tobacco, as she recalled Max's words on the subject—"But you never drink . . . Heaven knows . . . I've tried hard enough with you"—and then wryly commented on her abstemiousness: "Everyone struggles through life with some unfortunate disability. Mine is to be unable to appreciate either alcohol or tobacco" (Christie, *Come Tell*, 32). Given her reticence to publicly discuss her life and fiction, ostensibly one of Agatha's defining traits was her shyness, evident in her refusal to allow herself to be photographed to promote her novels and in her shunning of interviews: "I have never enjoyed interviews, which always make me feel embarrassed and tired, and why people should want to read articles about the author of books they have read, I have never been able to understand."[22] In similar self-deprecating fashion, Agatha declared, "Writing is a great comfort to people like me, who are unsure of themselves and have trouble expressing themselves properly" (Petschek, "Agatha Christie," 129). Yet how shy was she? For many shy people, shyness is not a perpetual condition in itself but a response to environmental conditions, evident in Agatha's assessment of her attempts to win the friendship of Mac, a new member of Max's archeological team, whom she feared would "prove [to be] one of those people who from time to time succeed in rendering me completely imbecile with shyness. I have, thank goodness, long left behind me the days when I was shy of *everyone*. I have attained, with middle age, a fair amount of poise and *savoir faire*" (Christie, *Come Tell*, 15). A. L. Rowse, Agatha's friend and a noted literary scholar, similarly commented on the interplay of the retiring and outgoing aspects of her personality. "She actually avoided publicity all she could, never gave an interview or made a speech, let alone appeared on TV," he acknowledged, as he further scrutinized the contrast between her public and private self: "she was so modest; her essential self so subdued and withdrawn in society; her persona as a writer was something quite different, almost as if there were two personalities."[23]

Furthermore, consider the cagey performance of identity that Agatha performs in her following "perverted" statement about Istanbul's Hagia Sophia: "I, alas, have never admired Sainte Sophie! An unfortunate lapse of taste; but there it is. It has always seemed to me the wrong size. Ashamed of my perverted ideas, I keep silent" (Christie, *Come Tell*, 12). Yet in proclaiming her silence over her "perverted" ideas, she speaks candidly of them—or, at least, of this particular one. All human beings experience both an interior and exterior life, and we can only grasp at their interiors through the exterior events witnessed by all and the interior events that they share with the world.

While reading an author's fiction for insights into her personal life has fallen out of fashion for many literary critics, such a perspective illuminates various aspects of Agatha's life and fiction. Most notably, Agatha casts a version of herself in her novels through the character of mystery writer Ariadne Oliver, with numerous points of congruency between the two. The name Ariadne refers to the clever Greek maiden who helped Theseus to escape the Minotaur's labyrinth, only for him to abandon her; this allusion captures Agatha's ability to create and solve literary mazes for her readers, while also echoing Archie's jilting of her. Like her creator, Ariadne Oliver is known for her apple-eating,[24] and Agatha famously tired of Hercule Poirot, as Ariadne tired of her Finnish detective Sven Hjerson: "I've written thirty-two books by now—and of course they're all exactly the same really . . . and I only regret one thing, making my detective a Finn. I don't really know anything about Finns and I'm always getting letters from Finland pointing out something impossible that he's said or done" (*Cards on the Table,* 51). Readers can discern innumerable such snippets of Agatha's life in her fiction. Max noted that Agatha found inspiration for her settings from actual landscapes, pointing out that the house of *Dead Man's Folly* resembles their home Greenway (*Mallowan' Memoirs,* 203). Christie found inspiration for her novels from a range of sources, including friends and family. For instance, Max stated that the character of Emmott in *Murder in Mesopotamia* is based on him (208), and it is likewise generally acknowledged that Katharine Woolley, wife of famed archeologist Leonard Woolley, inspired Louise Leidner, the first victim of this novel (208). One can only surmise the social repercussions of casting a family acquaintance as an imperious and nearly Machiavellian schemer who dies after a traumatic head injury.

While the circumstances and motivation behind Agatha's 1926 disappearance will likely remain forever murky, it is certainly notable that, in *Giant's Bread,* written during roughly the same period, one character remarks to another, "You've made a mystery about Groen [a musician]—part of your press campaign, I suppose" (11), which suggests Agatha's canny appreciation for the ways in which enigmas pique the interest of the public and the press. Also in *Giant's Bread,* another character, Vernon Deyre, suffers from amnesia: "The man was in a kind of mental fog. He knew his name and where he came from, but very little else" (274). In another striking coincidence that mirrors events from Agatha's life, Vernon Deyre assumes the name of George Green; George Chetwynd is the name of his rival for his wife's affections, as Agatha assumed the name of Nancy Neele during her 1926 disappearance. At the very least, Agatha recognized that mysteries and publicity enhance interest in artists, whether film stars, authors, or musicians, and after generating so much attention about herself, she never left the public eye for the remaining fifty years of her life.

Further along these lines, Agatha's novels illuminate the shifting historical circumstances of the twentieth century, which allows additional insights into her views of contemporary politics, whether regional, national, or international. For instance, J. C. Bernthal examines Agatha's depictions of women's bodies in such 1940s novels as *Evil under the Sun* and *The Body in the Library,* distilling the ways in which Hollywood films and prevailing notions of social class influence their presentation.[25] Nicholas Birns and Margaret Boe Birns observe that *They Came to Baghdad* and *So Many Steps to Death,* two of Agatha's novels from the 1950s, reimagine her earlier depictions of the Middle East, seeing it now as "a Cold War world in which national independence for Arab countries is on the horizon."[26] Along with such historical contextualizations of her fiction, John Curran's studies of Christie's writing process elucidate the ways in which her novels required extensive drafting and redrafting, in which she used "[her] Notebooks as a combination of sounding board and literary sketchpad"; such archival studies allow deeper insights into her constructions of her crimes and also of her responses to shifting cultural circumstances.[27] With at least one book published every year between 1920 and 1976 (with the odd exceptions of 1921 and 1943), Christie's novels depict the changing nature of twentieth-century life, providing a metaphoric photo album in which the advancing years and shifting cultural codes are registered.

To read Agatha's novels as reflective of aspects of her biography, despite the tut-tutting of some critics, illuminates her, them, and their shared historical moment. Readers do not require an understanding of authors' lives to digest and appreciate their fictions, but such knowledge invariably enlightens the reading experience, sparking insights that would otherwise remain hidden. In effect, reading Agatha's fiction through the events of her life and through her celebrity persona, creates, if not quite a mystery in itself, nonetheless another puzzle to be enjoyed as it is decoded, as readers piece together the autobiographical elements that intersect with the fictional ones. Thus, the paradox of Agatha Christie's biography is that it remains wholly superfluous yet integral to enjoying her fiction, an interpretive red herring that simultaneously allows a fuller comprehension of the mysteries at hand.

THREE

The Scofflaw of the Golden Age of Detective Fiction

Whether in retrospect the act should be considered a mere coincidence or an illuminating portent, Agatha Christie published her first novel, *The Mysterious Affair at Styles,* in 1920—the year that heralds the beginning of the so-called Golden Age of Detective Fiction, which reigned for the following two decades. For afficionados of the mystery novel, this era represents the genre's apex, its flowering from the seeds of decades past into a highly engrossing and increasingly sophisticated genre. As with most declarations of any so-called Golden Age, such a designation sutures over the conflicts waged before, during, and after these supposedly halcyon years, and in this instance, over the fraught nature of mystery novels as an aesthetic narrative form in themselves, particularly in relation to authors' debates concerning its proper contours. When viewed within the context of the Golden Age of Detective Fiction and of the decades preceding it, Christie's contributions to the genre come into sharper focus, as her novels both complement the general tenor of the era while resisting, even subverting, many of its established tropes and emerging dictates. Moreover, if one examines the history of the genre through Hercule Poirot's amateur pursuits as a literary critic, Christie's innovations in the field of detective fiction come into sharper focus. As all noted authors must do, Christie inherited a preexisting literary tradition that she then sculpted to her own needs and desires; she also refused to conform her novels to the increasingly rigid rules of the genre, thus fashioning herself into a literary scofflaw of prevailing and emergent conventions.

As the early history of detective fiction is often told, Edgar Allen Poe is credited as the progenitor of the genre with "The Murders in the Rue Morgue," a short story published in the April 1841 issue of *Graham's Magazine,* in which the investigator C. Auguste Dupin solves the mysterious murders of two women. In a metadiscursive meditation on this new direction for fiction, Poe envisions his protagonist and his readers as people of an analytical mindset, those who are "fond of enigmas, of conundrums, hieroglyphics" and who exhibit in their pursuit of a mystery's solution "a degree of *acumen* which appears to the ordinary apprehension præternatural."[1] Dupin appeared in two subsequent stories, "The Mystery of Marie Rogêt" (1842) and "The Purloined Letter" (1844). Subsequent entries in this emergent field include Emile Gaboriau's novel *L'Affaire Lerouge* (1866), often titled *The Widow Lerouge* in its English translation, identified as the first detective novel (or *roman policier*). Gaboriau's protagonist, Père Tabaret, while investigating the widow's murder, summarizes the logical precepts behind his investigation: "Given a crime, with all the circumstances and details, I construct, piece by piece, a plan of accusation, which I do not warrant until it is entire and perfect. If a man is found to whom this plan applies exactly in every particular, the author of the crime is found; otherwise, we have laid hands upon an innocent person."[2] Dupin and Père Tabaret, in their joint role as foundational detectives of investigative fiction, endorse logic and methodical analysis as their key methods for solving mysteries, in a trope that remains highly influential to the characters and plots of the genre.

Detective fiction soon immigrated to England with Wilkie Collins's *The Moonstone* (1868), and a decade later in the United States, Anna Katharine Green's *The Leavenworth Case* (1878) introduced Ebenezer Gryce, a detective following the Dupin and Père Tabaret model of investigation. The form skyrocketed in popularity with Arthur Conan Doyle's *A Study in Scarlet* (1877), which marked the debut of the iconic Sherlock Holmes, whose adventures continued in a series of successful publications, including *The Sign of Four* (1890), *The Adventures of Sherlock Holmes* (1892), and *The Memoirs of Sherlock Holmes* (1894). R. Austin Freeman's *The Red Thumb Mark* (1907) features the first scientifically based investigation, undertaken by Dr. Thorndyke, whereas G. K. Chesterton's *The Innocence of Father Brown* (1911) explores the psychological causes and effects of crime. Maurice Leblanc initiated his famed series featuring Arsène Lupin—simultaneously a gentleman, a thief, and a detective—in 1905. Gaston Leroux's *The Mystery of the Yellow Room* (1907) popularized the genre of the locked-room mystery, which he soon followed with his mysterious *The Phantom of the Opera* (1910), even if it is not precisely a mystery.

Every mystery writer must confront the legacy of Poe's Auguste Dupin and Doyle's Sherlock Holmes, and many authors therefore fashion idiosyncratic detectives, creating unique and memorable figures who distinguish their fictions from others. As Christie stated of her inspiration for Hercule Poirot and Miss Marple: "I was worried about finding a detective for my first book, and we'd had Belgian refugees at the beginning of the War, so I thought that quite a good idea. But I didn't really know any. Miss Marple, of course, is very like one's aunts or grandmothers."[3] On numerous occasions, Christie readily acknowledged her debts to Doyle and Sherlock Holmes, such as when Ariadne Oliver comments of Poirot: "He's a detective. You know. The Sherlock Holmes kind—deerstalkers and violins and all that" (*McGinty*, 80). Christie replaced "deerstalkers and violins and all that" with crème de cassis, an exorbitant moustache, and a variety of other foibles, yet the chief appeal of both characters—their ability to pierce through a confusing array of clues, red herrings, and conflicting testimony—unites them. Poirot further resembles Holmes in their methodical approach to investigations, evident when Poirot slightly misquotes his forebear: "I have my methods, Watson." ("Problem at Sea," *Regatta,* 182).[4] His deductive capabilities impress a range of characters, including one who asks admiringly, "Are you really a kind of Sherlock Holmes and do wonderful deductions?" ("Yellow Iris," *Regatta,* 93), and Poirot himself alludes to Sherlock Holmes, in a rather telling passage: "It reminds you of Sherlock Holmes, does it not? The curious incident of the dog in the night . . . Ah, well, I am not above stealing the tricks of others" (*Cards on the Table,* 69). Poirot refers here to Doyle's "The Adventure of Silver Blaze," in which Holmes solves the mystery because a guard dog does not bark,[5] but Poirot's suggestion that he is "not above the stealing the tricks of others" would imply that Christie allowed herself to be inspired by the works of her forebears in detective fiction.

Despite the strong connections between Holmes and Poirot, additional evidence suggests that Christie grew impatient with the comparison, and in these instances readers can discern her efforts to liberate herself from her predecessors. For instance, when Amy Leatheran, the narrator of *Murder in Mesopotamia,* meets Poirot, she is surprised that he does not accord with her image of a detective as inspired by Doyle: "I don't know what I'd imagined—something rather like Sherlock Holmes—long and lean with a keen, clever face" (*Mesopotamia,* 72). One of Christie's characters muses, "Personally, I myself think the Sherlock Holmes stories greatly overrated. The fallacies—the really amazing fallacies—that there are in those stories" (*Death in the Air,* 132), and the murderer of *Crooked House* dismisses Holmes as an avatar of a bygone era: "Anyway, I'm not very keen on Sherlock Holmes. It's awfully old fashioned" (110). In a similar instance Poirot snubs Doyle's plots while admiring his prose: "These tales of Sherlock Holmes are in reality far-fetched, full of fallacies and most artificially contrived. But the art of the writing—ah, that is entirely different. The pleasure of the language, the creation above all of that magnificent character, Dr. Watson" (*Clocks,* 112). Ironically, Poirot's disparagements of Doyle echo many critics' assessments of Christie's writings as offering outré and unconvincing plots enlivened by vibrant prose and dialogue. Most obviously, Christie emulated the pairing of Sherlock Holmes and Dr. Watson with Hercule Poirot and Hastings, even compelling Hastings to acknowledge his inferior narrative position by referring to himself as "the humble Watson" (*Poirot Loses a Client,* 28). Yet as many writers discover, what they first perceived as inspiring can metamorphose into a constricting force on their own imaginations, and Christie, finding the Watson figure unnecessary for her plots, thus dispatched Hastings: "I got very tired of Captain Hastings, Poirot's Watson. Quite early on I banished him to the Argentine."[6] This lesson appears to have been fully absorbed by 1930 when Christie introduced Miss Marple in her first novel, *The Murder at the Vicarage*: Miss Marple never requires a Dr. Watson figure as her sidekick.

As the example of Sherlock Holmes suggests, Christie immersed herself in the many authors of this literary legacy, also evident in the fact that Poirot enjoys in his retirement from the police force his new hobby of literary criticism. Poirot's most extensive forays in literary analysis occur in two of Christie's later novels, *The Clocks* (1963) and *Third Girl* (1966). Ironically, these two novels are often considered among the weaker of Christie's efforts: the reason behind the many clocks of *The Clocks* rings hollow, and Robert Barnard lambastes *Third Girl* as "one of Christie's more embarrassing attempts to haul herself abreast of the swinging 'sixties."[7] As is the case with so many of Christie's novels, even if in some or another way a given entry in her canon fails to fully satisfy, in another way it springs to life, and such is the case with Poirot's literary musings. In *Third Girl* Christie indicates that Poirot has long read detective fiction enthusiastically but critically, finding much to praise and much to condemn and that he has collected his thoughts in "his *Magnum Opus,* an analysis of great writers of detective fiction." She writes that Poirot "lauded to the skies two American authors who were practically unknown, and had in various other ways given honour where honour was due and sternly withheld it where he considered it was not. . . . He had enjoyed this literary achievement and enjoyed the vast amount of reading he had had to do, had enjoyed snorting with disgust as he flung a book across the floor . . . and had enjoyed appreciatively nodding his head on the rare occasions when such approval was justified" (*Third Girl,* 1). In his new pastime, Christie's detective finds fault with the genre's originators: "He had dared to speak scathingly of Edgar Allen Poe, he had complained of the lack of method or order in the romantic outpourings of Wilkie Collins" (*Third Girl,* 1). Continuing his appraisals, Poirot evaluates Maurice Leblanc's *Adventures of Arsène Lupin* in terms similar to his analysis of Doyle, in finding the plots farfetched yet the prose immersive: "How fantastic; how unreal. And yet what vitality there is in them, what vigour, what life! They are preposterous, but they have panache" (*Clocks,* 109).

In many instances, readers can glean insights into Christie's reactions to her critics by examining Poirot's literary criticism, and thus better perceive her accomplishments in the Golden Age of Detective Fiction as a whole. Poirot praises Green's *The Leavenworth Case* as "admirable," and, similar to Poe's Auguste

Dupin and Gaboriau's Père Tabaret, Green's Ebenezer Gryce modeled for Christie the type of logical mindset that defines the protagonist of the genre. "It is not for me to suspect but to detect," Gryce declares succinctly, and he later expostulates on his investigative methods: "Now it is a principle which every detective recognizes the truth of, that if of a hundred leading circumstances connected with a crime, ninety-nine of these are acts pointing to the suspected party with unerring certainty but the hundredth equally important act is one which that person could not have performed, the whole fabric of suspicion is destroyed."[8] Beyond these similarities between Gryce's and Poirot's *modi operandi*, Poirot further praises Green's novel, adding that "one savors its period atmosphere, its studied and deliberate melodrama" (*Clocks*, 109). These words also hint at Christie's impatience with criticisms of her works for their melodramatic qualities. For Christie, melodrama, which favors stock characters expressing over-pitched emotions, does not represent the failure of an incompetent neophyte but the intended effect of a seasoned author, one who purposefully pursues this technique for the audience response it generates. Sounding a similar note, Christie's contemporary John Dickson Carr allowed his protagonist, Dr. Fell, to defend the use of melodrama: "The point is, [authors] are afraid of the thing called Melodrama. So, if they can't eliminate the melodrama, they try to hide it by writing in such an oblique, upside-down way that nobody under heaven can understand what they are talking about."[9] In their defense of melodrama, Christie and Carr tacitly strike back against critics who denounce their works for such exaggerated emotionality, pointing out its utility and power for works of detective fiction. Also relevant to this point, the line between realism and melodrama can be surprisingly thin, as expressed in the assessment of one of Christie's characters to the odd events unfolding around her: "Melodramatic, but one does read of such things happening" (*Unexpected Guest*, 78).

In another instance of Christie rebutting her critics through Poirot's literary analyses, the detective singles out Gaston Leroux's *The Mystery of the Yellow Room* for unqualified praise. "That is really a classic! I approve of it from start to finish" (*Clocks*, 109), he effuses, as he then argues against the novels' critics: "There were criticisms of it, I remember, which said that it was unfair. . . No. All through there is truth, concealed with a careful and cunning use of words" (109). Here too readers can discern Christie responding to her critics, for she vigorously defended her novels against any accusations of "cheating the reader" with similar terms and rejected the accusation that she employed false clues, declaring instead: "I just say things that can be taken two ways . . . I don't cheat."[10] *Murder in Retrospect* illustrates Christie's doubled use of language, as the solution to the mystery hinges on the victim's words, "It's all settled—I'll send her packing, I tell you!" (182). These words are slightly rephrased in the novel's theatrical adaptation as *Go Back for Murder*—"All right, I'll send her packing"

(656)—but in both instances, the simple pronoun *her* likely leads many readers and audience members astray.

Emerging from this literary backdrop that ranged from the mid-nineteenth to the early-twentieth centuries, the Golden Age of Detective Fiction witnessed the evolution of the crime novel into an extraordinarily popular genre of increasing sophistication. Along with Christie, illustrious British names associated with this period include G. K. Chesterton, Ronald A. Knox, Michael Innes, and Edmund Crispin. Perhaps it is mere coincidence that the Golden Age of Detective Fiction overlapped with the enfranchisement of women in 1918 and 1928, following the passage of the Representation of the People Acts in the United Kingdom, for women authors had long achieved great success for their literary efforts. It is nonetheless striking that many of the most esteemed authors of the Golden Age of Detective Fiction are women. Margery Allingham, Dorothy Sayers, Ngaio Marsh, and Christie were dubbed the era's Queens of Crime, and such secondary figures as Patricia Wentworth, Gladys Mitchell, and Josephine Tey were widely celebrated as well. Beyond the borders of the British empire, American authors contributed notably to the genre's heyday, including John Dickson Carr, recognized as the master of the locked-room mystery; Earl Derr Biggers, author of the Charlie Chan mysteries; Erle Stanley Gardner, author of the Perry Mason mysteries; and Ellery Queen, the name of the fictional detective posing as the author of this eponymous series, which was penned by Frederic Dannay and Manfred Bennington Lee. Belgian author Georges Simenon found acclaim for his Jules Maigret mysteries.

Broadly speaking, the Golden Age of Detective Fiction prized the creativity and puzzle of the "whodunit," in which a crime, usually a murder, occurs; the detective, a person of superior intelligence, insight, and cleverness, investigates. The investigation typically features a series of interviews with witnesses; as these interviews unfold, the detective observes a slight contradiction in testimony, evidence, or other such details. As Poirot says, "It is very valuable, conversation. Sooner or later, if one has something to hide, one says too much"; in complementary contrast, he further explains: "There are the innocent people who know things, but are unaware of the importance of what they know" (*Cat among the Pigeons,* 175). Frequently the perpetrator is revealed with the remaining witnesses and suspects present, granting these surprising finales an audience amazed by the detective's ingenuity, with their response modelling the author's intended effect on the reader.

Within these general parameters, individual authors developed unique strategies for deceiving readers, and Christie's clever solutions evince her steady attention to the necessity of a well-designed puzzle as the heart of the story. The fuzzy demarcation between a puzzle and a mystery novel contributes heavily to the denigration of the genre, and such contemporaneous works as Lassiter

Wren and Randle McKay's *The Baffle Book* (1928) stripped detective fiction of its novelistic trappings and turned it into a parlor game, offering condensed accounts of mysteries with the reader charged with determining the solution and the answers printed upside-down in its final pages. Reflective of this publishing phenomenon, Christie's "The Plymouth Express" includes an editorial interruption similar in intent, stressing the story's puzzling elements: "*It is suggested that the reader pause in his perusal of the story at this point, make his own solution of the mystery—and then see how close he comes to that of the author.—The Editors*" (*Under Dog*, 79; cf. "The Affair at the Victory Ball," *Under Dog*, 96). In constructing her puzzles, and thus her novels, Christie reverse-engineered her plot—"You know, you start with the wish to deceive and then work backward"[11]—and thus wove a basic element of deception, predicated on her careful attention to words and the slippage between their meanings, into the resolution. As she proceeded backward from the story's resolution to its formulation, she often employed the key strategy of misdirection. Both Miss Marple and Hercule Poirot identify misdirection as an essential tactic of magicians, as they further explain its relevance to the mysteries at hand. Miss Marple declares: "Because if you're looking at one thing, you can't be looking at another. And one so often looks at the wrong thing, though whether because one happens to do so or because you're meant to, it's very hard to say. Misdirection, the conjurers call it" (*Murder with Mirrors*, 78). Hercule Poirot similarly affirms: "It was merely the trick of the conjuror. Misdirection. You focus the eyes on the kidnaping *here* and it does not occur to anyone that the kidnaping *really* occurred three weeks earlier in Switzerland" (*Cat among the Pigeons*, 199). Along with her title as the Queen of Crime of the Golden Age of Detective Fiction, Christie could be similarly dubbed Her Majesty of Misdirection.

But much as the people living during the Western Middle Ages could never have guessed that their era would later be dubiously posited as a "middle" between the classical era of Greece and Rome and the subsequent flowering—or perhaps grandiosity—of the Renaissance, the writers of the Golden Age of Detective Fiction lived in the moment of their literary production, not in the aftermath of its designation as the genre's apex. Opinions from this era diverged widely over the quality of the writing produced. Almost two decades before the Golden Age, G. K. Chesterton published "A Defence of Detective Stories" in 1902, in which he discerned a general prudery leveled against the genre: "The trouble in this matter is that many people do not realize that there is such a thing as a good detective story; it is to them like speaking of a good devil."[12] In his 1939 essay "The Golden Age of English Detection," John Strachey effusively celebrated the literary achievements of the form: "Here are books which the authors evidently enjoyed writing and the readers unaffectedly enjoy reading. I have myself little doubt that some of these detective novels are far better jobs, on any account, than are nine tenths of the more pretentious and ambitious high-brow novels."[13] Only two years after Strachey praised the literary achievements of the Golden Age of Detective Fiction, Philip Van Doren Stern lamented the degradation and decadence of the genre in his 1941 essay "The Case of the Corpse in the Blind Alley," arguing that it "needs overhauling, a return to first principle, a realization that murder has to do with human emotion and deserves serious treatment."[14] This essay is often credited as the death knell of the Golden Age of Detective Fiction, even though many of the authors associated with this period continued writing for decades, notably Christie herself. The interrogative titles of Edmund Wilson's 1944 essay "Why Do People Read Detective Stories?" and his 1945 essay, "Who Cares Who Killed Roger Ackroyd?" adequately convey his derogatory views both of Christie—"I hope never to read another of her books"—and of the genre of detective fiction altogether. In a biting analogy, he compares its afficionados to alcoholics: "Detective-story readers feel guilty, they are habitually on the defensive, and all their talk about 'well-written' mysteries is simply an excuse for their vice, like the reasons that the alcoholic can always produce for a drink."[15]

As much as the Golden Age of Detective Fiction is considered by many to represent the apex of the genre, one can hardly be surprised that several authors of the period did not recognize it as such. Indeed, it is a truth universally acknowledged that some writers write well while others write poorly, and the skyrocketing success of detective fiction in the 1920s also facilitated the publication of several works of dubious merit and frustrating plotting. In his 1924 essay "The Art of the Detective Story," R. Austin Freeman argued for the genre's aesthetic potential and optimistically assessed the groundswell among authors for more exacting standards for their art: "In late years there has arisen a new school of writers who, taking the detective story seriously, have set a more exacting standard, and whose work, admirable alike in construction and execution, probably accounts for the recent growth in popularity of this class of fiction."[16] Notably, Freeman mentions authors who "set a more exacting standard," presumably by and for themselves as individual authors, yet other writers attempted to prescribe such rules for all authors of detective fiction. In his 1928 essay "A Detective Story Decalogue," Ronald A. Knox, author of the Miles Bredon series, outlined a set of rules for the popular genre, in a *cri di coeur* against substandard entries in its growing canon:

1. The criminal must be someone mentioned in the early part of the story, but must not be anyone whose thoughts the reader has been allowed to follow.
2. All supernatural or preternatural agencies are ruled out as a matter of course.
3. Not more than one secret room or passage is allowable.

4. No hitherto undiscovered poisons may be used, nor any appliance which will need a long scientific explanation at the end.

5. No Chinaman must figure in the story.[17]

6. No accident must ever help the detective, nor must he ever have an unaccountable intuition which proves to be right.

7. The detective must not himself commit the crime.

8. The detective must not light on any clues which are not instantly produced for the inspection of the reader.

9. The stupid friend of the detective, the Watson, must not conceal any thoughts which pass through his mind; his intelligence must be slightly, but very slightly, below that of the average reader.

10. Twin brothers, and doubles generally, must not appear unless we have been duly prepared for them.[18]

Frustrated with the subpar plotting evident in supernatural events, houses with an improbable number of secret passages, and homicidal twins, Knox redirected writers of detective fiction to the art of plotting, of arranging their narratives with carefully constructed clues that lead to the culprit's identity. At their core, Knox's rules enumerate the panoply of ways that the *deus ex machina* was reimagined for detective fiction, and he urged authors to avoid such dodges. Writing in the same year, S. S. Van Dine, the pseudonym of Willard Huntington Wright and author of the Philo Vance mysteries, published an essay titled "S. S. Van Dine Sets Down Twenty Rules for Detective Stories." Van Dine doubled Knox's decalogue, making many similar points while contributing as well his personal bugbears. He rejected the intersection of mystery and romance ("There must be no love interest. The business in hand is to bring a criminal to the bar of justice, not to bring a lovelorn couple to the hymeneal altar") and insisted that the culprit be found among the higher social classes ("A servant must not be chosen by the author as the culprit. This is begging a noble question. It is a too easy solution"). Additionally, he rejected the demands of literary fiction for a streamlined reading experience: "A detective novel should contain no long descriptive passages, no literary dallying with side-issues, no subtly worked-out character analyses, no 'atmospheric' preoccupations."[19]

Complementing Knox's and Van Dine's efforts, the Constitution and Rules of the Detection Club similarly attempted to legislate the genre's fundamental precepts. This club, formed in 1930, gathered together the foremost English mystery writers of the day, electing G. K. Chesterton as its first president. Article 1 of its constitution stipulates as a condition of membership for potential authors "That he or she has written at least two detective-novels of admitted merit or (in exceptional cases) one such novel; it being understood that the term 'detective novel' does not include adventure-stories or 'thrillers' or stories in which the detection is not a main interest, and that it is a demerit in a detective-novel if the author does not 'play fair by the reader.'"[20] The "fair play rule" is often considered the foundational axiom of detective fiction, yet within the annals of detective fiction, fair play is often found in the eyes of the beholder. Initiates into the Detection Club swore an oath both tongue-in-cheek and serious, as they were required to reply "I do" to the following questions: "Do you solemnly swear never to conceal a vital clue from the reader?"; "Will you honour the King's English?"; and "Do you promise that your detectives shall well and truly detect the crimes presented to them, using those wits which it may please you to bestow upon them and not placing reliance on nor making use of Divine Revelation, Feminine Intuition, Mumbo-Jumbo, Jiggery-Pokery, Coincidence, or the Act of God?"[21] Beyond these legalistic statements of the guiding precepts of detective fiction, many writers included in their novels their own sense of its proper contours of plot and exposition, such as when Ellery Queen, in *The Siamese Twin Mystery*, dismisses detective stories featuring "secret societies and such tripe" because such explanations may appear in substandard fiction but "not in real life."[22]

While Knox, Van Dine, and many of the Detection Club's members surely aspired to encourage authors to write better stories by avoiding the genre's clichés, great fiction can be guided but never constrained by rules, and authors of the period chafed against such strictures. In *The Hollow Man*, John Dickson Carr includes a chapter titled "The Locked-Room Lecture," in which his detective, Dr. Fell, expostulates in a metacommentary on the detective novel. "We're in a detective story, and we don't fool the reader by pretending we're not," he begins, as he then refuses to encapsulate the tropes of the locked-room mystery into a quasi-legalistic code: "I am not going to start an argument by attempting to lay down rules." He later adds: "But when you twist this matter of taste into a rule for judging the merit or even the probability of the story, you are merely saying, 'This series of events couldn't happen, because I shouldn't enjoy it if it did.'"[23] In effect, Carr argues for the preeminence of the author and the reader for determining the success or failure of a given work, not the imposition of a code that can only constrain an author's ingenuity. Whether or not Christie read Knox's and Van Dine's rules, she, like Carr, certainly did not adhere to them. As Merja Makinen observes: "Christie's novels broke almost all of the gentlemanly Detection Club 'rules,' deliberately teasing the genre out of all recognition while ostensibly secure within its confines. In this sense, her novels encapsulate generic mobility . . . according to which crime fiction displays a 'transgressive impulse' thereby proclaiming and challenging its own limitations."[24]

Foremost, Knox's first rule, declaring that "the criminal . . . must not be any-one whose thoughts the reader has been allowed to follow," takes dead aim at Christie's *The Murder of Roger Ackroyd,* with his broadside published two years after her groundbreaking work. She repeated this "transgression" later in her career with *Endless Night*. Although the title character of the short-story collection *The Mysterious Mr. Quin* serves in the role of the detective / protagonist rather than as the culprit, Christie introduces "supernatural or preternatural agencies" throughout the works in which he appears, in direct opposition to Knox's second rule. It would appear that she adheres to Knox's tenth rule when she mocks the twin solution—"The identical twin solution? . . . So very convenient in fiction. But in real life, it doesn't happen you know" (*Pale Horse*, 92–93)—but she comes rather dangerously close to breaking it in such novels as *A Holiday for Murder* (although with half-brothers, not twins) and *A Murder Is Announced* (with sisters Letitia and Charlotte Blacklock). Ellery Queen may have dismissed "secret societies and such tripe," but Christie's *At Bertram's Hotel* features a criminal organization, with no detriment to this intriguing tale of murder and mayhem.

The following question arises: In considering the inherent implausibility of binding guidelines for fiction, who determines when a so-called rule is broken? Knox argues that "No hitherto undiscovered poisons may be used," but hitherto undiscovered by whom? The general reader is unlikely to know of the curious effects of thallium poisoning, a murderous device that Christie uses to great effect in *The Pale Horse*. Regarding Van Dine's rules, Christie eschews romance for her protagonists—with Hercule Poirot a confirmed bachelor and Miss Marple a spinster—yet many of her novels include a secondary plot of lovers overcoming obstacles to unite. For example, *Murder on the Links* features Hastings's romance, ending in eventual marriage, to "Cinderella." *The Murder of Roger Ackroyd* depicts the growing attraction of Flora Ackroyd and Major Blunt, and in *Elephants Can Remember* Celia Ravenscroft and Desmond Burton-Cox cannot marry until the shadow of Celia's parents' deaths has been cleared, with numerous other examples of such plotlines throughout her corpus. In her adaptations of her novels into plays, Christie rewrote certain plotlines, including those of *Towards Zero* and *Go Back for Murder,* so that they would end with romantic pairings; indeed, in the revised ending of the theatrical version of *And Then There Were None,* she revivifies two of the novel's dead characters and pairs them romantically. Christie typically limits her range of suspects to family members and friends rather than expanding it to include servants and employees, yet they play key roles in such works as *Ordeal by Innocence* and *Poirot Loses a Client.* Knox condemned mysteries solved by intuition rather than by evidence, but in some instances, Christie glides over the evidence necessary to convict the malefactors, such as in *The Murder at the Vicarage* when Colonel Melchett chastises Miss Marple, "Your solution is a very plausible one . . . but you will allow me to point out that there is not a shadow of proof" (222), and so they plot a trap to catch the killer. In the same novel, Miss Marple states, "I know that in books it is always the most unlikely person. But I never find that rule applies in real life" (215), and these words suggest her author's cagey reframing of one of the most common "rules" of detective fiction. Finally, Knox demands that "The detective must not himself commit the crime," yet Christie long planned for her career to conclude with this ultimate transgression, as she transforms Poirot into a murderer in *Curtain.* Indeed, after writing *Curtain* in the early 1940s, Christie alerted readers to her plans for Poirot in subsequent works. In *Mrs. McGinty's Dead,* a playwright proposes to Ariadne Oliver: "You know, Ariadne, that might be rather a marvelous idea. A real Sven Hjerson—and *you* murder him. You might make a Swan Song book of it—to be published after your death." Amusingly, Oliver replies, "What about the money? Any money to be made out of murders I want now" (126)—in a telling reference to Christie's troubles with the US and British tax authorities.

As Knox's and Van Dine's lists express their exasperation with overdone tropes of detective fiction, so do Christie's novels allow insights into her own assessments of the genre's and its authors' failings. *Death in the Air* features among its suspects Norman Clancy, "a writer of detective stories," for whom Inspector Japp expresses his disdain: "Set of ignorant scribblers! This is just the sort of fool murder that a scribbler of rubbish would think he could get away with" (8, 29). "Ignorant scribblers of rubbish": this telling formulation exposes Christie's exasperation with her less-talented peers. Poirot often refuses to investigate a crime scene, remarking that he will solve the mystery through logical deduction rather than through a superfluity of physical evidence; he does not require "the cigarette ash—nor the footprint—nor a lady's glove—nor even a lingering perfume. Nothing that the detective of fiction so conveniently finds" (*Thirteen at Dinner,* 58), and here he echoes Van Dine's impatience with "determining the identity of the culprit by comparing the butt of a cigarette left at the scene of the crime."[25] In plotting her novels, Christie limits herself to misdirecting readers through a single coincidence, but not multiple ones, evident when Hastings says to Poirot, "You said yourself once that one coincidence is nearly always found in a murder-case" (*Poirot Loses a Client,* 198), when Poirot concedes, "I am always prepared to admit *one* coincidence" (*Holiday for Murder,* 148), and when Miss Marple distinguishes for readers between real clues and a coincidence. "Oh, dear, no. . . . *That* wasn't a coincidence" (*Murder at the Vicarage,* 220), she explains of one vexing event, and then identifies the single truly random event: "That is what I call the coincidence" (222). Locked-room mysteries, known as the particular strength of Christie's contemporary John Dickson Carr, were also becoming somewhat clichéd, and although Christie availed herself of the tropes of this particular subgenre, such as in *Murder in Mesopotamia* and *Dead Man's Mirror,* she recognized that some of her readers might find it wearisome, evident in the words of Colonel Johnson in *A Holiday for Murder*: "Do you mean to tell me, Superintendent, that this is one of those damned cases you get in detective stories where a man is killed in a locked room by some apparently supernatural agency?" (*Holiday for Murder,* 69). As apparent virtually throughout the history of the arts and humanities as a whole, tropes once vibrant and exciting deaden into staleness through overuse, and writers must negotiate this tension to avoid devolving into the kind of hackneyed writing that Knox and Van Dine hoped to discourage.

This problem of overused tropes is exacerbated for genre fiction in the simple requirements that a romance novel must feature a romance, a science-fiction novel must feature futuristic technology, a detective novel must feature a mystery, and so on. These plot requirements are then complicated by the genre's standard parameters and further complicated in the amorphous realm between rules for authors and the expectations of readers. Anna Faktorovich explains this complex interrelationship: "The trouble with modern formulaic writing is not that it has too few rules, but rather that the rules are numerous and dictate the dimensions of elements that are much more complex than the boundaries they are allowed."[26] In other words, genre writing requires its authors to respect its boundaries, yet any such boundaries should not constrain authors from transgressing them in accord with their unique visions. Complicating matters further, the gender politics of these prohibitions should not be overlooked. As women like Christie increasingly entered the field of detective fiction, men like Knox and Van Dine increasingly attempted to delineate its contours. An enduring theme of myth and literature illustrates the consequences arising when women refuse to accept men's proscriptions on their behavior, and more specifically, on their quest for knowledge, in such stories as Pandora and Bluebeard's wife. Christie's resistance to rulebound fiction functions in similar terms, as she liberated herself from unnecessary constraints imposed by others.

And so as much as Christie enduringly reigns as the most popular author of the Golden Age of Detective Fiction, this period paradoxically fails to capture her comfortably within its parameters, and perhaps most notably in the simple fact that many of her greatest works were written after the 1930s. Furthermore, whereas most histories of detective fiction begin with Poe, traces of the form date back millennia, including the story of Susanna in Jewish scriptures, and Stephen Knight discerns the genre's foundational texts as William Godwin's *Things as They Are; or, The Adventures of Caleb Williams* (1794) and Charles Brockden Brown's *Edgar Huntly* (1799).[27] The Golden Age of Detective Fiction conveniently marks the beginning of Christie's career, which continued for an additional thirty-six years after this era's conclusion, and thus many of her masterworks highlight the arbitrariness of this construction. How Golden can a Golden Age be if it arbitrarily excludes Christie's *Murder in Retrospect* and *The*

Moving Finger for the crime of being written two years after the period's end? By breaking men's "rules" for detective fiction while adhering to her own sense of the genre's demands, Christie penned works that challenged any arbitrary efforts to curtail the possibilities of the genre, proving instead the deeper freedoms of genre fiction than many of its most esteemed practitioners imagined.

FOUR

The Hardboiled Queen of the Cozies

It has long been said that England and the United States of America are two countries divided by a common tongue, and this aphorism can be extended to the historic division between their conceptions of detective fiction, in the enduring generic binary between the "cozy" and "hardboiled" styles. While Agatha Christie and many of her compatriots of the Golden Age of Detective Fiction were English writers who came to be associated with the cozy tradition, across the Atlantic Ocean several American writers, notably Dashiell Hammett and Raymond Chandler, developed the hardboiled style of mystery novel. Along with her title as one of the Queens of Crime of the Golden Age of Detective Fiction, Christie is also frequently lauded as the Queen of the Cozies. "Cozies are detective stories in the tradition of Agatha Christie," writes Tom Leitch, thus positioning her as the inspiring wellspring for the authors of this subgenre.[1] Yet much as Christie's achievements are not fully contextualized, and even undervalued, by zealously linking her to the Golden Age of Detective Fiction, so too does her status as Queen of the Cozies minimize the full extent of her authorial vision. Capable of penning novels ranging in tone and tenor from the intellectually perplexing to the hair-raising, Christie eludes the constraints of the cozy / hardboiled binary while also exposing its gendered biases, again paradoxically proving the limitations of being dubbed a "Queen," no matter the compliment intended.

As the word *cozy* implies, this subgenre of mystery fiction is envisioned as comforting readers; it elicits images of them snuggling up in front of the fireplace, or curling up in bed, as they hold an engrossing book in their hands for a peaceful evening at home. Cheekily alluding to this image of cozy reading, Ellsworth Grant refers to Agatha Christie as "the best of all companions in bed,"[2] and Otto Penzler, owner of the Mysterious Book Shop in Manhattan, similarly opines: "Agatha Christie [is not] threatening to anybody. Picking up an Agatha Christie book is like putting on cuddly old slippers."[3] Cozy readers, it is presumed, desire a distraction from the vexations and troubles of their real lives and the world at large, and they thus relish the escapism offered through this genre of fiction, for cozies depict a narrative space where, although violence erupts in the form of a murder, readers can rest assured that the detective will restore order by the novel's end. As with Ronald A. Knox's and S. S. Van Dine's attempts to codify certain requirements and prohibitions of the mystery novel, critics such as Marilyn Stasio have documented the expected tropes of cozies:

> No gore. Violence is kept to a minimum and described discreetly.
>
> Amateur status is preferred in a sleuth, who is often a woman with an interesting occupation.
>
> The crime takes place close to home, or within a confined community in which the victim, suspects, and sleuth are all known to one another.
>
> The settings are never sleazy; the atmosphere is designed to give pleasure and comfort.
>
> The characters are driven by personal motivations and have no affiliation with institutions like the Mafia or the C.I.A.
>
> The hero does not get beaten up during the investigation, although romantic entanglements are permissible.[4]

Taken together, Stasio's precepts envision a genre that soothes, rather than agitates, its readers through a simple formula: a functional, although not altogether harmonious, social order is introduced; it is disrupted through crime, usually the murder of an unpleasant person over whom the other characters need not excessively mourn. Following the detective's investigation, the criminal is identified, and the social order is restored to its prior sense of comfortable stasis. Cozies are frequently aligned with women authors, readers, and characters, as indicated by Stasio's observation that this genre often foregrounds female detectives for its protagonists.

For the most part, Christie's mysteries adhere to Stasio's precepts. Her murderers typically commit their nefarious deeds with poisons or single gunshots, not with bloody stabbings, eviscerations, or disembowellings. Trained in the vagaries of human nature but not in the telltale clues of forensic analysis, Miss Marple belongs among the ranks of amateur investigators, and, as a retired detective, Hercule Poirot retains an air of professionalism yet without the status either of the Belgian police force or of Scotland Yard to bolster his authority. One might assume that, owing to its title, Christie's eponymous protagonist of *Mr. Parker Pyne, Detective* is, in fact, a professional detective; instead, this book features a retired governmental statistician, who, with his professional duties behind him, has decided "to use the experience I have gained in a novel fashion" (*Parker Pyne,* 2). Christie often sets her murders in closed environments such as estate houses or rural villages, with occasional forays onto trains (*The Mystery of the Blue Train*), planes (*Death in the Air*), and boats (*Death on the Nile*), although only very rarely does she descend into London's underworld or other potentially "sleazy" locales. Whereas several characters in Christie's adventure novels are affiliated with criminal or governmental institutions, such is not the case with her mystery fiction, except, as mentioned previously, the criminal organization behind the misdeeds in *At Bertram's Hotel.* And finally, and mercifully, it is true that neither Miss Marple nor Hercule Poirot are "roughed up by toughs" during the course of their investigations, although on one occasion Ariadne Oliver is attacked while pursuing a lead: "She hurried . . . down a narrow passageway, heard a footstep behind her, half turned, when she was struck from behind and the world went up in sparks" (*Third Girl,* 89). In contrast to Van Dyne, who proscribed romances in his essay "S. S. Van Dine Sets Down Twenty Rules for Detective Stories," Stasio permits them, although neither Miss Marple nor Hercule Poirot pursue love affairs while solving the mysteries they encounter—although it should be noted that Poirot expresses deep admiration for the mysterious Countess Vera Rossakoff. Acknowledging in an obituary the genial pleasures afforded by her fiction, the editors of *Christianity Today* thanked Christie for "provid[ing] millions of readers with hours of restful reading pleasure," with their words tacitly identifying her supreme place in the authors' pantheon of cozy detective fiction, and with little irony (as there need not be) in the editors of a Christian publication lauding the author of fictions that repeatedly break a rather significant admonition of the Ten Commandments: Thou shalt not kill.[5]

Opposed to the cozy stands the hardboiled mystery, which typically features a corrupt society overrun by organized crime; an ineffective, understaffed, and sometimes complicit police force; politicians seduced by graft; and an antihero protagonist with a wearied sense of ethics who fights for justice, if only reluctantly. As Christie's *The Mysterious Affair at Styles* in 1920 marks the dawn of the Golden Age of Detective Fiction, credit for the birth of the hardboiled mystery is typically dated to 1922 with the publication of Dashiell Hammett's first *Black Mask* story. Geoffrey O'Brien attests that, in comparison to the cozy's English roots, the hardboiled style is linked to the United States: "the characteristically cool and cynical tone of the tough-guy novels was a distinctly American invention."[6] Christie is forever linked to her detectives Hercule Poirot and Miss Marple, and so too are the progenitors of the hardboiled school eternally connected to their wearied protagonists: Dashiell Hammett's Sam Spade (*The Maltese Falcon,* 1930), Raymond Chandler's Philip Marlowe (*The Big Sleep,* 1939), and Mickey Spillane's Mike Hammer (*I, the Jury,* 1947), as well as such later authors and detectives as Sara Paretsky's V. I. Warshawski (*Indemnity Only,* 1982) and Walter Mosley's Ezekiel "Easy" Rawlins (*Devil in a Blue Dress,* 1990). Invented in the United States, the hardboiled school of fiction soon grew in international influence, with many readers entranced by its hard-knuckle approach to crime and criminals, as well as its subsequent influence on the nascent cinematic genre of film noir.

As the formula of the cozy mystery features the disruption and restoration of a functional social order, the formula of the hardboiled mystery novel could be similarly but distinctly posited as a world in which a dysfunctional social order is introduced; it is disrupted further through a particularly puzzling or otherwise egregious crime; following the detective's investigation, the criminal is identified; and the dysfunctional social order is restored to its prior status quo. As Tom Leitch notes of the contrasting dynamics of these genres: "The cozy concentrates on evoking a particular, apparently stable milieu that is disrupted by death; the hardboiled story presents a world in which death is normal, is indeed the defining condition of normalcy."[7] The antihero protagonists of hardboiled novels diverge notably from the precedents set by the likes of C. Auguste Dupin and Sherlock Holmes, and Helmet Heissenbüttel summarizes the distinctions between the two primary characterizations of detectives: "There is a classic pair of opposites among detectives: the one who, roughly or even brutally, thrashes his opponents (and naturally is himself also thrashed on occasion) until he has found out who done it; and the other who, by a mixture of investigation of facts and combinatory puzzle solving, brings what was at first confused and opaque into plausible connection and makes it transparent."[8] Sounding a similar note, Jerome Delamater and Ruth Prigozy assert that "the classic British detective story is based primarily on ratiocination. Its American counterpart, however, has from the outset been described as 'hardboiled.'"[9] In sum, cozy detectives interview, reflect, and deduce to solve mysteries; hardboiled detectives stand ready to brawl.

Christie denounced the hardboiled literary school on several occasions, declaring herself surprised and disappointed by its popularity: "No one could have dreamed then that there would come a time when crime books would be read for their love of violence, the taking of sadistic pleasure in brutality for its own sake" (*Autobiography,* 424). Allusions to hardboiled fiction, often disparaging in tone, appear regularly in her novels, and notably in Poirot's reactions to current novels and films. After Poirot spends the evening at home rather than attending the cinema, the narrator reports his reasoning: "Scenes of violence and crude brutality were the fashion and as a former police officer, Poirot was bored by brutality. . . . He found it fatiguing, and unintelligent" (*McGinty,* 3). When a character asks Poirot about "the tough school" of detective fiction, he replies coolly: "Violence for violence's sake? Since when has that been interesting?" (*Clocks,* 111). Indeed, occasional characters appear to have ingested so much hardboiled fiction that they view the United States as hopelessly depraved, as in the words of a maid interviewed by Poirot: "I've read about Chicago and them gunmen and all that. It must be a wicked country; and what the police can be about, I can't think. Not like our policeman" (*Thirteen at Dinner*, 68). It is equally plausible that this maid refers to Chicago's real-life criminal underbelly, as notoriously led by Al Capone, but in either instance, this city represents the violent antithesis of the cozy tradition's small villages and manor houses. As with so many thematic issues across Christie's extensive corpus, one can find countervailing opinions, and her overriding distaste for the hardboiled school is complicated by the fact that she depicts Miss Marple as a reader of such fiction. When Miss Marple uses the term *fall guy*, she explains that she herself reads these novels—"I got it from one of Mr. Dashiell Hammett's stories"—as Christie then ventriloquizes a compliment to her fellow author of mystery fiction: "I understand from my nephew Raymond that he is considered at the top of the tree in what is called the tough style of literature" (*A Murder Is Announced*, 74).

While any binary division too strongly linking the cozy style with English writers and the hardboiled style with American writers would inevitably collapse owing to the many cross-pollinations of authors and styles on both sides of the Atlantic, it is well worth pondering why *cozy* should describe any murder mystery. As Susan Rowland notes, the term *cozy* "indicat[es] a paradoxically comforting quality to stories about catching murderers. Cozies feel 'cozy' because they end in a restoration of a relatively tranquil social group whose values are strengthened by *one of their own* solving the murder."[10] True, but *one of their own* is typically the murder victim (or victims) as well, and *one of their own* is typically the murderer, too. These conditions hardly seem conducive to the *gemütlich* tenor for which the so-called cozy genre ostensibly strives. Furthermore, the distinction between cozy and hardboiled mysteries carries with it an overarching (and oversimplified) gender politics, one that aligns the former with femininity and the latter with masculinity, with these words themselves hinting strongly at their gendered undertones. G. M. Malliet, herself a writer in the cozy tradition, acknowledges this word's potentially alienating effect: "I think *cozy* is a kind of twee word that makes some men flee in horror."[11] But most importantly in considering Christie's literary reputation, authors of the cozy school are rarely acknowledged for their literary artistry and innovation, whereas several authors of the hardboiled school are increasingly viewed as trailblazing talents, as evident in David Madden's assessment of Raymond Chandler's burgeoning literary reputation: "Since his death in 1959, Raymond Chandler has been elevated to detective fiction's pantheon of writers and many scholars have even ventured to argue that Chandler's is an important voice in twentieth-century fiction, without qualifying this achievement by noting that he worked in popular fiction."[12] As in so many other instances, women's work—or work simply associated with women—is devalued in comparison to similar work undertaken by men. And so we may well ask, what does the binary between cozy and hardboiled fiction accomplish, other than to devalue artworks associated with women authors such as Agatha Christie?

Even as much of Christie's fiction falls within the parameters of the cozy tradition as outlined by critics, in several notable moments she adopts a dark, menacing, and distinctly discomforting tone, which additionally undercuts any taxonomic value of the cozy / hardboiled binary. For instance, as much as Christie refrained from depicting violence for the sake of violence, one should not lose sight of the fact that, whether a novel depicts a murder by arsenic poisoning or by a gunshot to the head, the victim remains equally dead. Christie dulled the visceral impact of murder in many novels, yet she accentuates it in others, such as in the rising body counts of *And Then There Were None* and *Death Comes as the End.* Indeed, if one tallies the murders of *And Then There Were None* committed both by the killer and by the killer's victims in the novel's backstory, the body count reaches into the dozens. In the dedication of *A Holiday for Murder,* Christie responded to the genial criticism of her brother-in-law James Watts and promised a truly gruesome murder: "*You complained that my murders were getting too refined—anaemic, in fact! You yearned for a 'good violent murder with lots of blood.' A murder where there was no doubt about its being a murder!*" (*Holiday for Murder* dedication page). Christie delivered in her promise, evident in Poirot's reaction to the crime scene: "Yes, that is it—*violence.* . . . And blood—an insistence on *blood.* Blood on the chairs, on the tables, on the carpet. . . . Such a frail old man, so thin, so shriveled, so dried up—and yet—in his death—*so much blood*" (*Holiday for Murder,* 74). Other elements of Christie's novels that challenge the concept of coziness include the séance and death ritual scenes of *Pale Horse* (150–54), the psychological torment suffered by the Boynton family in *Appointment with Death,* and the child murders in both *By the Pricking of My Thumbs* and *Hallowe'en Party,* among many other chilling and unsettling scenes. Her short story "The Last Séance" features a medium "birthing" a deceased child back to life and the mother stealing it away, leaving the medium dead in a shrunken husk of her former body; this tale, which includes a pseudo-scientific explanation of paranormal phenomena, illustrates Christie's interest in tropes and traditions of the horror genre (*Double Sin,* 168). One should not overinterpret a chance use of the word *cozy* as necessarily referring to the cozy / hardboiled binary, but it is nonetheless instructive to consider the scene when, after Detective Inspector Hardcastle learns that characters are drinking tea to calm themselves after discovering a murder, the narrator reports, "Dick's comment was that it all sounded very cozy" (*Clocks,* 11). It is difficult to interpret this statement without irony. In complementary contrast, one of the characters of Christie's play *Verdict* describes the murderer as "much too hard-boiled" (553), which further blurs any binary between these two styles within her corpus.

Also aligning Christie with the cozy tradition, several of her titles, and thus her plots, are inspired by children's nursery rhymes, notably *And Then There Were None; One, Two, Buckle My Shoe* (aka *The Patriotic Murders*); *Five Little Pigs* (aka *Murder in Retrospect*); *Crooked House; Three Blind Mice* (aka *The Mousetrap*); *Mrs. McGinty's Dead; A Pocket Full of Rye;* and *Hickory Dickory Dock* (aka *Hickory Dickory Death*).[13] Any simplistic assumption that children's literature exclusively features narratively comforting themes is itself highly debatable, and so too should any assumption that Christie's novels based on children's verse are inherently cozy in their plotlines. Illustrating these points, Christie's novels were frequently retitled for publication in the United States, and it is evident that her American publishers sought to stress the murders of *One, Two, Buckle My Shoe* and *Five Little Pigs* by renaming them *The Patriotic Murders* and *Murder in Retrospect;* in effect, the publishers were attempting to market these books as less cozy and, if not precisely as hardboiled, certainly as more violent than children's verse would suggest. At the same time, by aligning her murderous plots with light rhymes that readers likely remember from childhood, she alienates her audience from any previous expectation of the rhymes' meanings, metamorphosing the familiar and innocuous into the unfamiliar and deadly. Of these titles, *And Then There Were None* and *A Pocket Full of Rye* most effectively link the fates of the nursery rhyme characters to those of Christie's characters, creating eerie parallels that suggest not merely the murderousness of the respective killers but their depraved obsession with staging fanciful jingles within the real-life settings they inhabit. In *Murder in Three Acts*, playwright Muriel Wills discusses her new production, titled *Little Dog Laughed*, and describes it as "a kind of modern version of the nursery rhyme—a lot of froth and nonsense—hey-diddle-diddle and the dish-and-the-spoon scandal," to which Sir Charles agrees, "The world nowadays is rather like a mad nursery rhyme" (*Three Acts*, 145). Inverting children's rhymes into murderous plots, Christie creates a determinedly alienating effect from many readers' beloved memories of childhood verse.

Efforts to pigeonhole Christie's novels as cozy and escapist fare are also undercut by her frequent references to well-known murderers of the past, thus interweaving elements of nonfiction into her fictional (and purportedly escapist) worlds. She alludes to a range of notorious cases, often to enhance the suspense of her novels by likening her unfolding plots to actual events. With its depiction of a potential serial killer stalking the citizens of England, *The ABC Murders* surely stands as one of her less cozy mysteries, and as one character nervously states, "It's like Jack the Ripper all over again" (*ABC Murders*, 130, 194; cf. *Cat among the Pigeons*, 179). Notably, the identity of Jack the Ripper remains an unanswered question, imbuing this scene with a similar sense of disquiet. Christie repeatedly refers to the case of Hawley Harvey Crippen (*Murder in*

Retrospect, 45; *Labors of Hercules,* 37; "Tape-Measure Murder," *Three Blind Mice,* 99; *Sleeping Murder,* 59), an American living in England who, in 1910, murdered his wife Cora but then explained her absence by claiming that she had returned to the United States. In *The Patriotic Murders* Inspector Japp, conversing with Poirot, alludes to the gruesome case of Isabella Ruxton in 1935, who was murdered by her husband, a physician afterwards dubbed the "Savage Surgeon." Japp proposes that a missing woman might have met a similar fate: "I suppose you're hinting that . . . we'll find her in a quarry, cut up in little pieces like Mrs. Ruxton?" (*Patriotic Murders,* 81). A character in *Cat among the Pigeons* refers to Thomas Neill Cream, the serial killer known as the Lambeth Poisoner, suggesting that, as Cream "went about killing an unfortunate type of woman" in the 1880s and 1890s, the murderer in this novel "just goes about killing schoolmistresses" (*Cat among the Pigeons,* 179). (The "unfortunate type of woman" alluded to among Cream's victims were mostly prostitutes and women seeking abortions.) Perhaps what is most unsettling about the so-called Brighton Trunk Murders of 1934, alluded to in *The Body in the Library* (93) and *The Labors of Hercules* (142), is that the murders of an unidentified woman and of Violette Kay were unrelated; this macabre coincidence led Brighton to be dubbed "The Queen of Slaughtering Places."

Complementing these murderous men and their female victims, Christie alludes to a wide range of murderous women, thereby balancing the gender politics of her true-crime allusions. In the 1850s Madeleine Smith was suspected of murdering her boyfriend Pierre Emile L'Angelier, but insufficient evidence precluded her conviction for the crime; in *Sleeping Murder,* Smith is cited as an example of "a type who commits a crime, manages to get away with it, and is darned careful never to stick a neck out again"—which parallels the actions of the novel's culprit (*Sleeping Murder,* 32; cf. *Pale Horse,* 172). Christie repeatedly cites the most infamous of unconvicted but likely murderers, Lizzie Borden, particularly as an example of the impossibility of predicting people's behavior: "Such apparently unlikely people do the most fantastic things. Take the case of Lizzie Borden. There's not really a reasonable explanation of that" (*Moving Finger,* 114; cf. *Ordeal by Innocence,* 37 and 48; *Elephants Can Remember,* 55; *Sleeping Murder,* 32 and 88). In 1860, sixteen-year-old Constance Kent slashed the throat of her four-year-old half-brother. She is alluded to in *Crooked House:* "Constance Kent, everybody said, was very fond of the baby brother she killed. . . . I think people more often kill those they love, than those they hate. Possibly because only the people you love can really make life unendurable to you" (103). In its attention to a family with relatively young children in the characters of Eustace and Josephine Leonides, *Crooked House* thematizes the possibility of violence meted out to and enacted by children. In the early 1920s, Edith Thompson plotted the murder of her husband Percy with her boyfriend Frederick

Bywaters; both Thompson and Bywaters were hanged for the crime. Thompson is described as a woman who "had lived in a world of violent unreality," an eerie but apt assessment of her and her crime that imbues the search for the murderer of *Funerals Are Fatal* with a similar frisson of dark fantasy (*Funerals Are Fatal*, 56; cf. *McGinty*, 91).

Also in *Funerals Are Fatal,* the lawyer Mr. Entwhistle muses over a rogues' gallery of true-crime killers: "Murderers as far as he could judge seemed to be of all sorts and kinds. Some had had over-weening vanity, some had had a lust for power, some, like Seddon, had been mean and avaricious, others like Smith . . . had had an incredible fascination for women; some, like Armstrong, had been pleasant fellows to meet. . . . Nurse Waddington had put her elderly patients out of the way with businesslike cheerfulness" (56). Frederick Seddon murdered his boarder Eliza Mary Barrow in 1911, and George Joseph Smith, a bigamist, was convicted for the Brides in the Baths Murders of 1912 to 1914. Herbert Rowse Armstrong murdered his wife by arsenic poisoning in 1921 and also attempted to murder Oswald Martin, a professional rival; to this day Armstrong remains the only solicitor to be executed for murder in England. In 1935 Dorothea Waddingham—not Waddington—killed a patient in her care to gain an inheritance. This laundry list of murderers creates a chilling effect, with readers confronted with the likelihood of untimely and violent death interrupting the tranquility of life in a range of everyday encounters, including those with their beloved family members.

As much as Christie alludes to famous murderers of the past to generate a sense of unease among her readers, with her novels approaching a greater sense of verisimilitude despite their obvious fictionality, she is also sufficiently versatile to reframe these true-crime accounts in a less threatening manner—in effect, to metamorphose the horrors of true crime into fodder for humor. Magda Leonides, one of Christie's flamboyant actress characters, hopes to stage Edith Thompson's story as a comedy: "I know they say I must always play comedy because of my nose—but you know there's quite a lot of comedy to be got out of Edith Thompson" (*Crooked House*, 36–37). In another lightly comic moment, Poirot cites several famous historical murders as a point of pride, confident that he could solve mysteries that perplexed the police and the public for decades: "There is no doubt whatever in my own mind who murdered Charles Bravo . . . Then there was that unfortunate adolescent, Constance Kent. The true motive that lay behind her strangling of the small brother whom she undoubtedly loved has always been a puzzle. But not to me. . . . As for Lizzie Borden, one wishes only that one could put a few necessary questions to various people concerned" (*Clocks*, 108).[14] This passage indicates Poirot's superior knowledge, in that he can solve the unsolvable crimes of the past, and thus it contributes to Christie's humorous motif of Poirot's egotism. Yet Poirot's musings are simultaneously somewhat disquieting because he withholds his theories from readers. The crimes thus remain unsolved and unsettling for them, and thus provide another strong example of how Christie's fiction dismantles the frameworks of cozy and hardboiled fiction.

Further tapping the power of true-crime incidents to bolster her fictions, Christie modeled several of her plots on real-life events, as Anne Powers documents through detailed readings of historical cases and Christie's fiction. Powers links the violent life of Dr. William Palmer, also known as the Rugeley Poisoner and the Prince of Poisoners, to the events depicted in *The Mysterious Affair at Styles.* The notorious Madame Marguerite Steinheil was reported to be having sex with French president Félix Faure when he died unexpectedly in 1899; subsequently, she was tried but not convicted for the murders of her mother and husband in 1908. Steinheil claimed that intruders gagged and bound her, a plot point employed in *Murder on the Links.* Pondering the far-reaching consequences of the kidnaping and murder of Charles Lindbergh's baby for his family, friends, and associates, Christie envisioned the revenge fantasy of *Murder on the Orient Express,* devising one of her most clever solutions as a satisfying resolution to this notorious case. Powers argues that the Hawley Harvey Crippen case parallels the plot of *Mrs. McGinty's Dead,* in that "the eternal-triangle story of fictitious Alfred Craig, Mrs. Craig, and Eva Kane equates to that of true-life Dr. Crippen, Cora Crippen and Ethel Le Neve, and is chiefly elucidated through Hercule Poirot's brief retrospective rumination on the fictional event."[15] George Joseph Smith's lethal mix of bigamy and murder matches key aspects of the killer's motivation in *A Caribbean Mystery.* As Powers argues of these and other parallels, while Christie's fictions reflect "her own unique and imaginative set of puzzles and solutions," these works "are also distinguished by an underlying authenticity lent by consideration of famous real-life crimes."[16]

Christie's interweaving of true-crime events into her novels testifies to her interest in building the credibility of her murders and thus in imbuing them with a disquieting edge, as does her interest in the nascent field of psychology. Somewhat paradoxically, Christie's novels gain emotional depth through their surface engagement with issues of psychology. Certainly, she is not attempting to plumb the depths of her individual characters' consciousnesses, as her contemporaries Henry James and Virginia Woolf did for their protagonists. Owing to the peculiar mandates of mystery fiction, such an objective is hardly possible because Christie would have needed to generate psychological portraits for all of her credible suspects, not merely for her protagonists, which would overwhelm her novels with character portraits to the extent that their mysteries would be lost. Further to this point, as Joan Acocella declares, complex psychological portraits would, almost by necessity, resolve the novels' mysteries: "If [Christie] had given her characters any psychological definition, we could have solved the mystery.

But as long as they are kept suspended, opaque—as they must be, in order for the book to be a puzzle—any one of them could be the culprit."[17]

Notwithstanding these limitations to the utility of psychology for detective fiction, this science and Christie's preferred genre matured during roughly the same period, as Amy Yang observes: "Both psychoanalysis and modern detective fiction evolved into their modern form around the turn of the twentieth century." One can readily see their overlaps and mutual interests: the psychoanalyst employs the tactics of the detective, interviewing and discussing with patients the roots of their neuroses or related troubles, whereas the detective employs the insights of the psychoanalyst, trying to frame a mental picture of the type of person who would commit the crime under investigation. Yang further posits: "With the introduction of the unconscious mind into mainstream discussion, psychoanalysis offered a concept more intriguing than just the obvious, surface motive."[18] Sigmund Freud rose to fame during Christie's childhood and teen years with the publication of *The Interpretation of Dreams* (1899) and *The Psychopathology of Everyday Life* (1904). He published many of his most trailblazing works in the 1920s, as she was breaking into the upper ranks of detective fiction: *Beyond the Pleasure Principle* (1920), *The Ego and the Id* (1923), and *Civilization and Its Discontents* (1930). In occasional passages, Christie offers a quick primer on psychology, which suggests the necessity of educating some readers on this emerging field. For example, in "The Red Signal," a short story published in *The Witness for the Prosecution,* a character explains the subconscious: "Your conscious self did not notice or remember, but with your subconscious self it was otherwise. The subconscious never forgets. We believe, too, that it can reason and deduce quite independently of the higher or conscious will" (27). The discovery, or the invention, of the subconscious afforded the opportunity for people to reconsider their understanding of their motivations and desires, and thus the possibility of discovering their own sense of alienation from themselves.

When employed effectively, psychology can dissolve any borders between the cozy and hardboiled styles, both of which are often more concerned with surface motivations for murder—greed, desire, revenge, corruption—than the possibility that the killer suffers from a psychological imbalance. Psychology, in effect, multiplies the potential number of suspects, for a given character need not be pursuing an outwardly apparent objective in dispatching the victim. Certainly, Christie tosses in many potential complexes for her characters, including the possibility of a "protection complex" (*Easy to Kill,* 73), an "inferiority complex" (*Easy to Kill,* 167), a "persecution complex" (*Cat among the Pigeons,* 98), and "incipient persecution mania" (*Sleeping Murder,* 137), as well as the supposition that a suspect has "a punishment complex—has had it, I suspect, since infancy" (*Funerals Are Fatal,* 200). "Sex mania" might motivate a killer (*Sleeping*

Murder, 159), as might the possibility that a killer is afflicted with a form of "religious insanity [that] made her feel that she had a divine command to rid the world of certain people" (*Pricking*, 133). One of Christie's more compelling armchair psychologists, Mr. Satterthwaite, even mentions "our Anglo-Saxon complexes" (*Three Acts*, 44), thus pathologizing the English as an inherently unbalanced people. In an absorbing example of the intersection of true crime and psychology, Mr. Satterthwaite assesses the roots of Crippen's criminality: "An inferiority complex is a very peculiar thing. Crippen, for instance, undoubtedly suffered from it. It's at the back of a lot of crimes" (*Three Acts*, 105). Such armchair diagnoses appear frequently in Christie's fiction, and one character is lightly satirized as "an excellent example of the danger of half-baked psychological theories in the head of an amateur" (*Towards Zero* Cast of Characters).

While one could easily dismiss such characters for their surface understanding of human psychology, Poirot perceives it as an essential component of his investigative technique. "I study the psychology of crime" (*Thirteen at Dinner*, 131), he declares, and notably as well, Christie employs his interest in psychology to distinguish him from detectives of the Sherlock Holmes model: "It is the psychology I seek, not the fingerprint or the cigarette ash" (*Orient Express*, 52). As the greatest detectives must master psychology, so too do Christie's more accomplished criminals understand the motivations of the human mind, as remarked upon by Mr. Parker Pyne: "If a criminal were a psychologist, what a criminal he could be" (*Parker Pyne*, 154). His words point to the necessity of understanding the complexities of human thought to better evade the strictures of human society. Christie's use of psychology, like her references to historical murderers, frequently creates an alienating and unnerving effect, in the simple fact that no one can fully understand the mental processes of another, even those to whom they are most intimately linked. As a character muses in *Murder in Three Acts*: "Some books that I've read these last few years have brought a lot of comfort to me. Books on psychology. It seems to show that in many ways people can't help themselves. A kind of kink" (106). In a fictional world where everyone might suffer from, or indulge in, a "kind of kink," or is otherwise characterized by a mental abnormality, any line dividing the psychologically stable and the psychotic is dizzyingly blurred.

To designate Agatha Christie as Queen of the Cozies is to unnecessarily delimit the scope of her accomplishments and to perpetuate stereotypes concerning the gendered preferences of women authors and their readers, and thus to do so latently calls into question the common critical practice of labeling authors as participants in certain writerly schools. Christie's contemporary James M. Cain, known for such riveting novels as *The Postman Always Rings Twice* (1934) and *Mildred Pierce* (1941), rejected the hardboiled label for himself and his fiction in the preface to *The Butterfly* (1947): "I belong to no school, hardboiled or otherwise, and I believe these so-called schools exist mainly in the imagination of critics, and have little correspondence in reality anywhere else. . . . If he can write a book at all, a writer cannot do it by peeping over his shoulder at anybody else, any more than a woman can have a baby by watching some other woman have one. It is a genital process, and all of its stages are intra-abdominal; it is sealed off in such fashion that outside 'influences' are almost impossible."[19] In a reversal of traditional gendered imagery, Cain compares himself to a woman giving birth, but one who must do so on her own, and the power of literature often arises in its ability to resist regimes of gender and genre. The cozy / hard-boiled binary latently encodes traditional gender roles into the creation and consumption of detective fiction, whereas much of the pleasure of the murder mystery arises in the novelty that a given author infuses into this narrative paradigm. Indeed, Christie began writing her novels before the terms *cozy* and *hardboiled* were applied to mystery fiction, which thus raises the paradoxical question of how one could be the queen of a genre she never envisioned.

FIVE

The Poet of Genre Fiction

How do we define the distinction between literary fiction and genre fiction? Critics know it when they see it, though they are hard-pressed to define it, for it is virtually impossible to circumscribe the aesthetic bliss of the former and the purported limitations of the latter. Furthermore, while it stands as one of the overarching goals of this chapter to render this binary ridiculous by exposing its useless prejudices, it is virtually impossible to extricate analysis of Christie's fictions from this divide, for the history of her books is also the history of their interpretation through this lens, particularly because she applied it to herself and her fictions. Christie did not shy from appraising her reputation as an author of genre fiction with sardonic good humor, referring to herself as "the mistress of low-brow detection."[1] In a more extended meditation on her career in the literary arts she similarly downplayed her achievements: "I drifted into writing. I tried music first—piano and singing. Then I wrote a story, and had it accepted by a magazine. That encouraged me. I think I've written seventy-five books. I'm a regular sausage factory. You can write anywhere, thank goodness! It must be awful to be a sculptor."[2] Why should one think of an author who compares herself to a sausage factory—grinding down the meat and marrow of a story through an imaginary mill until the product is extruded ready for consumption—as an artist, when she herself appears so amenable to devaluing her accomplishments? Christie's fellow Queen of Crime, Dorothy Sayers, similarly downplayed the aesthetic possibilities of their preferred genre: "It [the detective story] does not, and by hypothesis never can, attain the loftiest level of literary achievement"[3] With Christie, Sayers, and other writers of detective fiction diminishing their personal accomplishments and their chosen métier, any neutral, let alone positive, appraisal of the genre and its authors' achievements must overcome this defensive crouch built into the discussion. Even if one conceded the arguments of Christie's naysayers and agreed that her fiction lacks aesthetic merit, her literary style and narrative techniques surely affected her reception and thus illuminate why she remains one of the mostly widely read English-language authors in history.

Within longstanding, virtually sacrosanct, assessments of literary value, poetry occupies the opposite, and esteemed, end of the literary spectrum from detective fiction. Only the most outrageous and least credible of iconoclasts would claim that all poetry fails in its aesthetic objectives, thereby denying any worth to the works of such greats as Alexander Pope and Phillis Wheatley, Langston Hughes and Adrienne Rich; in contrast, several critics, including those quoted previously in this volume, blast all of detective fiction as inherently worthless. Given these conditions, it is instructive to recalibrate Christie's achievements by contextualizing her narrative structure and prose style through her poetic efforts, even though most readers view Christie primarily as a novelist and perhaps secondarily as a playwright.

Both of these perspectives overlook her interest in poetry, the field in which she first notched impressive accolades. Considering an early poetic effort, she dismissed her aesthetic achievements—"*Could* anything be more suggestive of a complete lack of literary talent?"—but she soon surpassed these juvenile attempts and published several poems over a decade prior to *The Mysterious Affair at Styles:* "By the age of seventeen or eighteen, however, I was doing better. . . . I sent one or two poems to *The Poetry Review.* I was very pleased when I got a guinea prize. After that, I won several prizes and also had poems printed there" (*Autobiography*, 179). Over the course of her career she published two collections of poems—*The Road of Dreams* in 1924 and *Poems* in 1973—as well as *Star over Bethlehem and Other Stories,* a collection of short stories and poems, in 1965. The eponymous protagonist of her play *Akhnaton* devotes his life to the arts and poetry, and many of his lines are written in verse, in contrast to the other characters who speak only in prose. With reviews parallel to the critical drubbing meted out to her detective fiction, several critics have lambasted her poetic efforts; Michael Holquist tersely denounced them as "vile."[4] At the same time, Christie's attention to poetry throughout her life contradicts any reductive assumption that she typed, rather than crafted, her sentences. Again creating a dialectic tension between an assumed binary, this time between the high arts of poetry and literature and the purportedly low art of genre fiction, Christie negotiated the limitations of the murder mystery, particularly in regard to its inherent restrictions on settings, characters, and plots, while imbuing her stories with a rich aesthetic depth and style.

To begin to address these issues in Christie's fiction, it is helpful to ponder what precisely is accomplished by presuming—or enforcing—a binary division between genre fiction and literary fiction. Critics have long viewed the two modes hierarchically, as John Cawelti explains: "Because such formulaic types as mystery and adventure stories are used as a means of temporary escape from the frustrations of life, stories in these modes are commonly defined as subliterature (as opposed to literature), entertainment (as opposed to serious literature), popular art (as opposed to fine art), lowbrow culture (as opposed to highbrow), or in terms of some other pejorative opposition."[5] The most provoking of these distinctions aligns genre fiction with entertainment, which thus implies that "serious literature" might very well not entertain its readers, an assumption that belittles the achievements of many great authors. In a similar vein, Ken Gelder distinguishes between popular and literary fiction by stressing the former's status "as 'entertainment,' its self-identification as a form of industrial production or 'manufacture,' and its commercial and merchandizing potential," in contrast to which literary fiction is valorized as "more complicated, resisting ideological reduction, disfavoring its commercial identity, able to criticize rather than capitulate to capitalism, enmeshed in nothing less than life itself."[6] Such capitalistic critiques in the debate between genre fiction and literary fiction are almost risible: surely most authors of literary fiction would be quite pleased if more readers purchased their books and thus padded their royalties. Some readers will prefer Stratford-upon-Avon and its productions of Shakespeare's plays over Universal Orlando's Wizarding World of Harry Potter and its re-creations of J. K. Rowling's fantasy fictions, but in a very real sense, both are theme park versions of the narratives—literary for the former, genre fiction for the latter—upon which they are based.

Assessing Christie's place in these debates, Chris Ewers summarizes the double bind facing authors of genre fiction and the myopic vision of the critics attempting to uphold it: "Academic critics, in a dubious critical move, have classified Christie as a 'lowbrow' author, the type of writer who is devoured and then forgotten; conversely, they compensate writers of greater weight for their lack of sales by emphasizing how *influential* they are. By a reverse logic, the more you are read, the less impact you have."[7] Adding another wrinkle to this critical imbroglio, the imaginary line dividing genre fiction from literary fiction is further blurred by the concept of middlebrow literature. Nicola Humble defines this mediating genre as "one that straddles the divide between the trashy romance or thriller on the one hand, and the philosophically or formally challenging novel on the other: offering narrative excitement without guilt, and intellectual stimulation without undue effort." Considering the detective novel as a subset of middlebrow literature, she adds, "the detective story forms an exception to the usual run of middlebrow novels; its ratiocinative elements offer . . . the illusion of an active, intellectually engaged reading, rather than a passive abandonment."[8] But why, one might wonder, does the middlebrow detective novel, or any novel, project "the *illusion* of an active, intellectually engaged reading"? Might this genre of fiction not actually provoke active, intellectually engaged reading? As the discussion of Raymond Chandler in the previous chapter mentions, some authors once dismissed as genre authors have metamorphosed into literary fiction authors, or are at least more widely respected than their first reviewers would have predicted. Passing the test of time, as writers such as Harriet Beecher Stowe and Bram Stoker have achieved, is perhaps the surest way for a writer's reputation to gain respect denied them during their lifetimes.

Christie's writing is often faulted for her style, a chorus that she joined when comparing herself to her contemporaries in the field of literary fiction: "If I could write like Elizabeth Bowen, or Muriel Spark or Graham Greene, I should jump to high heaven with delight, but I know that I can't, and it would never occur to me to copy them" (*Autobiography*, 394). Bowen, Spark, and Greene evince their unique styles as writers, yet their individual accomplishments do not preclude Christie's ability to articulate a style unique to her and to detective fiction. As Jean-Jacques Lecercle argues, style is "an ambiguous, if not a paradoxical, concept. It designates singularity in language . . . but it also designates the language or the artistic practice of a group."[9] Christie's idiosyncratic style is key to her appeal as a mystery writer, and it is also directly relevant to many attacks against the quality of her prose. Her writing—succinct, precise, and direct—represents her realization that the genre benefits from a quick pace: "Economy of wording, I think, is particularly necessary in detective stories" (*Autobiography*, 329). In an intriguing passage relevant to her own fiction, Christie recalls her mother's words about Sir Walter Scott's lengthy novels: "All these descriptions . . . Of course they are very good, and literary, but one can have too many of them" (*Autobiography*, 136–37). Christie eschewed such longwinded descriptive passages, and in *Unfinished Portrait,* her semi-autobiographical novel, the author Celia discloses that she "found local colour extremely elusive" (223). Celia's publisher admonishes her: "You'll never write well about anything you really know about, because you've got an honest mind. You can be imaginatively dishonest but not practically dishonest. You can't write lies about something you know, but you'll be able to tell the most splendid lies about something you don't know" (235). Christie's "honest mind" accepted her strengths and weaknesses as a writer, and she leaned into her strengths rather than wringing her hands over her weaknesses. One can readily imagine Christie's novels running many pages longer if she described in detail the furnishings of Styles, or waxed rhapsodic over the currents of the Nile, or lavished eagle-eyed attention on any number of her other settings or characters, but it is more difficult to imagine how such changes would improve her novels.

Brevity is acknowledged as the soul of wit, not as the animating impulse behind great fiction, but brevity is key to Christie's style. More so, she would have likely written even briefer novels had her publishers not encouraged her to write longer ones, as she noted: "I think myself that the *right* length for a detective story is fifty-thousand words. I know this is considered by publishers as too short" (*Autobiography*, 329). Further concerning the ideal length of mystery fiction, she added, "The short-story technique, I think, is not really suited to the detective story at all" (*Autobiography*, 329). Such a statement may to some degree surprise her readers, for not only did Christie write numerous short stories and short-story collections, but she also developed some of her masterworks from plots originally written in short-story format: *Death on the Nile* evolved from "Death on the Nile," a short story in *Mr. Parker Pyne, Detective; Evil under the Sun* evolved from "Triangle at Rhodes," a short story in *Dead Man's Mirror*. Still, the short-story format precluded Christie from drawing together a full cast of characters and left her less room to arrange her clues and red herrings.

Christie's novels benefit from her succinct style, and it is also apparent that she considered the aural quality of her words and sought to imbue them with a fresh, ear-catching flair. In plucky moments of metadiscourse, her characters comment favorably on her writing, such as when a character approves of the title of the book in which he appears: "Good title that, by the way. Lord Edgeware Dies. Look well on a bookstall" (*Thirteen at Dinner*, 96). Likewise, in *The Secret Adversary*, Tommy Beresford speaks to Tuppence and comments on the quality of his (and thus Christie's) words: "Remember that if Mr. Brown is all he is reported to be, it's a wonder that he has not ere now done us to death. That's a good sentence, quite a literary flavour about it" (42). Despite the tut-tuttings of certain critics, many of Christie's novels do indeed evince "quite a literary flavour" about them, highlighting her keen attention to language. She has an ear for the alliterative and an eye for the outré, evident in the mention of the "Californian Cucumber King's wife" (*Parker Pyne*, 15). Her metaphors often hit the mark, as in such phrases as "the kind of speculative interest she might have accorded to an odd sort of beetle" (*Death on the Nile*, 216) and her terse characterization of "the bluff breeziness of the ex-Naval man" (*Dead Man's Mirror*, 87). Occasional inversions of word order create memorable turns of phrase, as in the following: "Merciless, these modern young women, and terrifyingly alive" (*Murder in Three Acts*, 23). Even many of Christie's disparaging critics acknowledge her ear for dialogue, evident in such passages as "If a girl couldn't fend for herself a bit, I don't know where we'd all be" (*Death in the Air*, 115) and the following concise assessment: "That was stupid, but you are a stupid man" (*Holiday for Murder*, 195).

In fully evaluating Christie's style, it must nonetheless be conceded that she succumbed to the allure of clichés—the bane of the literary writer—frequently. To look at a few examples, a car is described as "running like a dream" (*Seven Dials Mystery*, 35), and a character finds that "words failed her" (*Seven Dials Mystery*, 204). Another character is "jumpy as the proverbial cat" (*Peril at End House*, 15), with the unnecessary word *proverbial* underscoring Christie's use of aphorisms. In one instance Poirot declaims in the manner of an aphoristic thesaurus: "There are many of your English idioms that describe him. The rough diamond! The self-made man! The social climber!" (*Evil Under the Sun* 125–26). A nonnative speaker of English, Poirot frequently employs clichés: "'For somewhere,' said Poirot to himself, indulging in an absolute riot of mixed metaphors, 'there is in the hay a needle, and among the sleeping dogs there is one on whom I shall put my foot, and by shooting the arrows into the air, one will come down and hit a glass house!'" (*McGinty*, 42). As Poirot's words evince, even clichés can produce a pleasing literary affect when used self-consciously, as further evident when the narrator wryly comments on Poirot's reliance on clichés—"One thing leads to another, as Hercule Poirot is fond of saying without much originality" (*Labors of Hercules*, 151)—which indicates Christie's interest in developing Poirot's character through his clichéd speech. In another instance, a character muses, "The world was at his feet. A phrase, but a good phrase" (*Why Didn't They Ask Evans?* 35), which indicates that Christie realized she was employing a cliché but chose it regardless as an apt expression of her character's perspective. Also, through their very overuse, clichés and aphorisms allow insight into the foibles of human nature, which stands as one of the enduring themes running across Christie's fiction, as evident when her ancient Egyptian character Esa voices such bromides as "Handsome is as handsome does" and "There's no fool like an old fool" (*Death Comes*, 17). When a character suggests, "First . . . we synchronize our watches," the narrator reports, "This familiar literary phrase had a heartening effect" (*At Bertram's Hotel*, 47). Surely Christie's fiction would have achieved a stronger literary flavor if she edited out overused idioms, yet it is worth considering as well that she employed them to achieve such "heartening effects." When a character muses over the phrase (and thus the title) *Easy to Kill*—"No wonder those words stuck in your mind. . . . They'll stick in mine—all my life!" (171)—readers hear Christie's attention to evocative phrases, even ones that had lost their luster of freshness.

Christie employs her direct, crisp style to immediately engage the reader in her fictions, thus merging her diction with the narrative tactic of hooking the reader's interest. One of Captain Hasting's narrative musings illustrates Christie's attention to hooks:

> I believe that a well-known anecdote exists to the effect that a young writer, determined to make the commencement of his story forcible and original enough to catch and rivet the attention of the most blasé of editors, penned the following sentence:
>
> "Hell!" said the Duchess. (*Murder on the Links*, 7)

There Is a Tide . . . similarly snags readers' attention with a brief statement likely recognized as a universal truth by anyone who has ever participated in a social organization—"In every club there is a club bore" (1)—and *The Moving Finger* immediately plunges readers into the mystery at hand: "I have often recalled the morning when the first of the anonymous letters came" (1). It would be difficult to resist reading the paragraphs that follow this simple but engrossing opening sentence.

Moving forward from the minefield that questions of style and aesthetics so often detonate, it is apparent that literary fiction and genre fiction differ markedly in a key way: Literary fiction is remarkably unbound by expectations of plot, style, and narrative conventions, whereas genre fiction must to some degree adhere to the conventions of the given genre. That is to say, the only requirement for literary fiction is that the characters, settings, plots, and themes be deemed sufficiently engaging or otherwise absorbing to win the reader's attention and praise, whereas successful genre fiction must similarly meet these minimal requirements while adhering to the restrictions of its particular field. Too often genre fiction is assessed according to the parameters of literary fiction; only very rarely is literary fiction assessed according to the parameters of genre fiction. As Michael Holquist argues, detective fiction must be reappraised according to its unique particularities: "The detective story's sketchy characters, its narrow settings, its rejection of mimesis in the service of structure all reveal themselves now as a quite proper—and sophisticated—lust to know its own discourse"; he adds further that the genre "consists of an austere, minimalist purity of narrative in which the story is the discovery of its own plot."[10] Precisely because murder mysteries revolve around the narrow circumstances of an enigmatic death, an investigation, and a resolution to this mystery, their characters, settings, and plots must be tailored to these requirements, despite the likelihood that these characters, settings, and plots, virtually by definition, will appear markedly dissimilar from those of literary fiction. As with those critics who snubbed Christie's style without adequately considering the terse aesthetics of the mystery novel, others have criticized her characters, settings, and plots without sufficient attention paid to the generic constrains placed on them.

In a key line of critique against genre fiction, its characters are denounced as hollow figures with little interiority, such that they can be condensed solely to their narrative functions. Raymond Chandler dismissed much detective fiction (and thus tacitly praised his more hardboiled style) by criticizing its characters: "to get the surprise murderer you fake character, which hits me hardest of all, because I have a sense of character."[11] To see Christie's characters as "fakes," however, misunderstands the foundational premise of the murder mystery, in which all characters must be approached as if they might be cloaking their motives for murder. Mystery novels require three roles—the victim, the killer, and the detective—with additional suspects and miscellaneous individuals rounding out the cast of characters. Critics such as Julian Symons contend that many mystery novelists strip their characters of personalities to accentuate their pivotal functions in the unfolding plots: "In constructing the detective story as a perfect mechanism, however, the Golden Age writers sacrificed almost everything else. Their work pandered to the taste of readers who wanted every character de-gutted so that there should be nothing even faintly disturbing about the fate of victims or murderers."[12] Symons oddly claims that readers of murder mysteries are squeamish about the murders depicted within the genre, and thus authors protect their readers from any emotional attachment to their characters. Any such barrier between readers and characters, however, more accurately represents the author's need to obscure their multiple characters' multifarious and often unstated objectives, rather than any predetermination that readers should not be discomforted by the murder of a fictional being.

Further to this point, and within the rudimentary distinction between flat and round characters, Christie's characters would ostensibly merit critique because they are uniformly flat. Along these lines, the vast majority of the detectives and inspectors who attempt to solve the crimes alongside Miss Marple appear interchangeable and virtually indistinguishable, and only the most devoted of Christie's readers could meaningfully distinguish between Superintendent Nash in *The Moving Finger* and Inspector Curry in *Murder with Mirrors,* or others of their ilk. Their narrative purpose is the same: to be outshined by Miss Marple's brilliance. In *The Complete Christie: An Agatha Christie Encyclopedia,* Matthew Bunson describes one of these men as "a discreet officer who does not seek headlines" and the other as "approach[ing] the problem with calm and confident efficiency," but does it matter which is which?[13] The name of Detective Inspector Bland of *Dead Man's Folly* rightly suggests that he is a rather forgettable, and thus aptly named, character. Even many of Christie's recurring characters evince little maturation over the course of their appearances. Colonel Race appears in four novels—*The Man in the Brown Suit, Cards on the Table, Death on the Nile,* and *Remembered Death*—but he is sketched vaguely and with little individuality: "Race was an out-of-door man, essentially the empire builder type—most of his life had been spent abroad" (*Remembered Death,* 89). Similarly, Dr. John Stillingfleet first surfaces in "The Dream" of *The Regatta Mystery,* is mentioned briefly in *Sad Cypress,* and more than twenty-five years later emerges for his third (and final) outing in *Third Girl.* After assisting Poirot with his investigations, Stillingfleet's storyline concludes with his engagement to Norma Restarick, the woman who enigmatically claimed to Poirot that she might have committed a murder at the novel's onset. Other than his impending nuptials, Stillingfleet's multiple appearances do not converge in a triumphant narrative arc, or culminate in a deep emotional insight, or any typical marker of a fully rounded character.

Relevant to these insights, while Hercule Poirot and Miss Marple exhibit strikingly different personalities, they share precisely the same narrative function—to solve the mystery that perplexes all other characters—and thus, because of this symmetry of purpose, it is quite possible to imagine, for example, Miss Marple solving *The Murder on the Orient Express* while vacationing abroad (as later occurs in *A Caribbean Mystery*) or Hercule Poirot solving *The Body in the Library* (or any other mystery set in an English village or manor house). Moreover, neither Hercule Poirot nor Miss Marple shifts notably before readers' eyes. They advance in years from old to even older, evident in the transitions for the former from *Cat among the Pigeons* to *Hallowe'en Party* (in which one character says of Poirot, "I don't think that one can rely on the faculties of a man of that age"; 196) and for the latter from *A Caribbean Mystery* to *Nemesis,* but they do not reach deeper insights into the human condition than they previously realized. Poirot enters the world as a retired detective, continues the work of a detective in retirement, and does not radically shift his worldview in any way. No emotional development is evident in the miniscule changes in his character, such as when he replaces his "large turnip-faced watch of earlier days" with a "neat wrist-watch" ("The Dream," *Regatta,* 126). His repeated mantra, "I do not approve of murder" (e.g., *Sad Cypress,* 89), while laudable, does not exhibit higher level moral or philosophical thinking, with the singular exception of the storyline of *Curtain,* in which he must become a killer to stop a killer. Miss Marple solves crimes owing to her detailed understanding of various personality types—"It's just that living in a village as I do, one gets to know so much about human nature" ("Strange Jest," *Three Blind Mice,* 74), she states—which has left her with a rather jaundiced view of humanity as a whole: "Miss Marple seldom gave anyone the benefit of the doubt; she invariably thought the worst, and nine times out of ten, so she insisted, she was right in so doing" (*At Bertram's Hotel,* 85). Beyond the fact that Hercule Poirot and Miss Marple exhibit little emotional development, they live inherently implausible lives, as Miss Marple realizes: "No, it has just happened that I have found myself in the vicinity of murder rather more often than would seem normal . . . I do not like to write it down, but it does appear that murders seem to happen in my vicinity" (*Nemesis,* 54). Hercule Poirot and Miss Marple, from this perspective, represent flat characters incapable of development or growth, whose repeated encounters with murder leave them just short of farcical, in terms of their believability as fully developed characters reflective of the human condition.

One might well ask in reply, why must characters experience emotional growth to be viewed as fully engaging, sympathetic, and recognizably human characters? Evaluating varieties of characters over centuries of literature, Robert Scholes and Robert Kellogg conclude, "The concept of the developing character who changes inwardly is quite a late arrival in narrative,"[14] and one can list numerous characters of literary classics who do not notably shift in their perceptions of the world: Odysseus, Beowulf, the knights of the Arthurian legend. More so, in a discussion of *Hamlet* in *The Rose and the Yew Tree,* Christie recognized that dynamic characters reflected a shift in narrative conventions: "Hamlet, with his musings, his 'to be or not to be,' was an entirely alien figure to his age. So much so that then and for long afterwards critics wrote condemning *Hamlet* as a play because of the fatal weakness of plot. . . . It is quite unbelievable to them that there could be a play about character" (93). Thus, Christie acknowledges this key shift in the historical construction of fictional characters, which suggests as well her understanding of the necessity of creating characters not out of deference to the aesthetic preferences of her age but to the narrative needs of her fiction. Expanding on related points, E. M. Forster, in his classic study *Aspects of the Novel,* encourages readers to appraise characters not according to universal parameters but to the idiosyncratic standards of a particular piece of fiction: "a novel is a work of art, with its own laws, which are not those of daily life, and . . . a character in a novel is real when it lives in accordance with such laws."[15] The characters of detective fiction must "live in accordance with such laws," those upon which the genre depends and those by which Christie's characters abide.

These converging viewpoints demonstrate that a virtually insurmountable challenge for writers of mystery fiction is to create characters who fulfill their narrative function—as suspects in a murder mystery—and who embody the complexity of fully developed human beings. Whereas realist literary fiction is often lauded for the lifelike portrayals of its characters, the basic premise of a murder mystery demands a roster of characters who would conceivably kill their enemies—mercifully, a grossly unrealistic prerequisite for real life, in which most of us can travel home for a holiday dinner without any real fear of murder disrupting the festivities, even if we occasionally squabble with our parents and siblings or hold on to unexpressed hopes for a generous inheritance. Christie recognized the inherent implausibility of creating lifelike characters for her novels, ventriloquizing her views through her alter-ego Ariadne Oliver: "Say what you like, it's not natural for five or six people to be on the spot when B is murdered and all to have a motive for killing B—unless, that is, B is absolutely madly unpleasant and in that case nobody will mind whether he's been killed or not, and doesn't care in the least who's done it" (*Pale Horse,* 11). That is to say, the mystery novel simultaneously requires verisimilitude, in that the events could plausibly occur in real life, while also requiring a cast of inherently implausible characters, any one of whom might be a killer.

Stock characters play a vital role in murder mysteries, and Christie did not shy away from employing them in her fiction, as evident in the cast of characters of *So Many Steps to Death,* in which she identifies three successive characters as either "typical" or a "type":

MRS. CALVIN BAKER—A typical American woman tourist—talkative, energetic, curious. Maybe she's even *too* typical.

JANET HETHERINGTON—Another type: the dour English traveller plagued by currency restrictions. Her knitting suffers, but she keeps a sharp eye about her.

HENRI LAURIER—Surely he's typical, too: A Frenchman bent on being gallant and charming and making small talk about the weather.

At the same time that mystery writers often employ stock characters, readers know they can never trust any character's description at face value. The sketch of Mrs. Calvin Baker warns, "Maybe she's even *too* typical"—and thus perhaps the character's surface presentation does not align with her deeper interiority. Yet if a character's surface presentation does not align with a deeper interiority, the framework of the stock character has been fractured. Part of the mystery of a mystery novel, therefore, is determining which characters are stock characters and which assume the mien of a stock character to camouflage their true identity as the villain—another role that might be dismissed as a stock figure but that requires sufficient motivation for the mystery to remain credible.

Furthermore, Christie realized that any emotional development that her characters might be expected to experience occurred in the narrative time prior to the commencement of her novels. In the prologue of *Towards Zero,* solicitor Mr. Treves—soon to be dispatched by the murderer—regales his audience with his views on criminology: "I like a good detective story . . . But, you know, they begin in the wrong place! They begin with the murder. But the murder is the *end.* The story begins long before that—years before sometimes—with all the causes and events that bring certain people to a certain place at a certain time on a certain day" (xi; cf. Christie's play *Towards Zero,* in which Mr. Treves expresses similar sentiments; *The Mousetrap and Other Plays* [*TMAOP*], 491). As Mr. Treves perceives, the inciting experiences that mold a human being into a murderer are almost uniformly undepicted in detective fiction, and thus static characters stand as virtually a prerequisite of the genre—but only if the reader is so incapacious and unimaginative as not to envision the potential evolution of an ordinary person into a murderer. As Anna Katharine Green explained of her characters and their misdeeds: "Crime must touch our imagination by showing people, *like ourselves,* but incredibly transformed by some overwhelming motive."[16] Given these principles, it could be posited that detective fiction, rather than curtailing readers' imaginations through the use of stock characters, activates their imaginations as they disentangle characters' back stories which, to some degree, require their furtive disclosure, even to the point of dissembling.

As Christie fashions a range of intriguing characters within the parameters of detective fiction, so too do her settings evince the particular challenges of the genre and her wily negotiation of them. For all fiction, whether genre or literary, settings serve the essential purpose of grounding the characters in a recognizable time and place. Even when characters resist the customs and mores of their locations, settings establish the necessary backdrop for their actions. Readers may encounter a locale unfamiliar or unknown within their personal experiences, yet the author must then communicate its essential features so that they understand its landscape, its culture, and its inhabitants. Indeed, the very concept of regional literature is predicated on the principle that it is virtually impossible to imagine some narratives transported to unfamiliar soils. One almost suffers from whiplash imagining Toni Morrison's novels set in eighteenth-century England or Flannery O'Connor's short stories set in the twenty-first-century American West.

Christie's novels, however, rely on regionalism for their quintessential Englishness while the settings themselves are virtually interchangeable, even when Christie leaves England altogether. Whether a particular victim is dispatched on the Blue Train or on the Orient Express, whether at the youth hostel of *Hickory Dickory Death* or at Bertram's Hotel, or in any one of Christie's nearly identical English manor houses or estates, the setting is essential yet oddly superfluous, rarely rising above the level of a simple backdrop. On many occasions, Christie viewed her settings in a utilitarian manner and minimalized their specificity. For instance, when she abandoned her primarily English settings for *Murder in Mesopotamia,* her narrator, Amy Leatheran, advises readers that they will see very little of the regional landscape: "I think I'd better make it clear right away that there isn't going to be any local color in this story. I don't know anything about archaeology and I don't know that I very much want to" (34)—a point Christie echoes in her autobiography *Come Tell Me How You Live*: "there will be no beautiful descriptions of scenery, no treating of economic problems, no racial reflections, no history" (xiv). With *Death Comes as the End,* Christie relocated her standard mystery plot both geographically and chronologically, yet as she explained in her "Author's Note," the setting is curiously insignificant to the mystery at hand: "The action of this book takes place on the west bank of the Nile at Thebes in Egypt about 2000 B.C. Both places and time are incidental to the story. Any other place at any other time would have served as well" ("Author's Note"). *Death Comes as the End* could have been set in Alexandria in 300 B.C.E. or in Baghdad in 800 C.E., or for the most part, even in England in the 1940s, with mostly surface edits. The characters' relationships would remain the same, the motivation for the many murders would remain the same, even if the widow Renisenb might be renamed Mary and the Nile replaced by the Thames in deference to the transposed setting.

Christie acknowledged that critics faulted her for frequently setting her novels in country estates, and her reply to this point suggests her slight impatience with critiques from those who did not recognize the peculiar demands of murder mysteries and again expected her to write her novels with the freedoms granted to authors of literary fiction. As she explained, "The one thing that infuriates me is when people complain that I always set my books in country houses. You *have* to be concerned with a house: with where people are. You can make it a hotel, or a train, or a pub—but it's got to be where people are brought together. And I think it must be a background that people will recognise, because explanations are so boring. If you set a detective story in, say, a laboratory, I don't think people would enjoy it so much."[17] One might well reply that a laboratory could serve admirably as the setting of a murder mystery. For example, this hypothetical laboratory could be helmed by an imperious researcher and populated with a gaggle of graduate students and interns murderously intent on taking credit for a breakthrough discovery that promises ample financial rewards and international renown. Christie's counterpoint would likely be that, even within such a setting, a pseudo-scientific and detailed description of this laboratory would simply divert attention from the novel's investment in the characters' emotional responses, to the extent that one of them metamorphoses into a murderer. Finally, it must be acknowledged that, whereas her settings play a rather negligible and background role in most of Christie's novels, *They Came to Baghdad* effectively employs its setting in Baghdad. This novel thus demonstrates by counterexample that Christie envisioned appropriate settings for her fiction by recognizing the varying degrees to which a setting influences a given genre.

In an amusing moment touching on the challenges of plotting murder mysteries, Inspector Japp comments on mystery novelist Daniel Michael Clancy, one of the suspects in *Death in the Air:* "I don't think it's healthy for a man to be always brooding over crime and detective stories. Reading up all sorts of cases. It puts ideas in his head." Poirot dryly replies, "It is certainly necessary for a writer to have ideas in his head" (63). In her detailed plotting Christie exceeded the achievements of so many other writers precisely because, in a transposition of their respective qualities, literary fiction requires emotionally resonant characters in a finely drawn setting, yet the plots of these novels might be rather minimalistic. For example, in their attention to the emotional development of their protagonists, many bildungsromans are extolled as literary masterpieces, including Jane Austen's *Emma* (1815), Charlotte Brontë's *Jane Eyre* (1847), D. H. Lawrence's *Sons and Lovers* (1913), Jeanette Winterson's *Oranges Are Not the Only Fruit* (1985), and Diran Adebayo's *Some Kind of Black* (1997). The plots of these novels, however, are typically episodic, allowing insights into the characters but without the necessity that the various plot points click together like a piece of clockwork on the final page.

Even though Christie was criticized for using "narrative simply as a way of structuring the detective puzzle," such a critique is virtually meaningless, for how can one write a detective story without using narrative as a way of structuring the detective story?[18] Instead, it is more helpful to recognize that mystery novels require specific narrative structures, as Pierre Bayard theorizes: "The detective thriller does not function as a seamless whole but works in two successive movements. The first of these, which lasts for most of the book, is a movement of *opening meaning* and tends to multiply leads and solutions. . . . The second movement, which intervenes at the end of the book, is a movement of *foreclosing meaning*. It brutally eliminates different possibilities and privileges a single one, charged with clarifying all proposed mysteries in retrospect while giving the reader the feeling that it was there in front of him all the time, protected by his blindness."[19] R. Austin Freeman, author of the Dr. Thorndyke mysteries, likewise focuses on the necessity of the conclusion for cogently completing a mystery novel, such that no other ending could appear to fall into place so convincingly: "To the critical reader the quality in a detective story which takes precedence of all others is conclusiveness. It is the quality which . . . yields that intellectual satisfaction that the reader seeks; and it is the quality which is the most difficult to attain, and which costs more than any other in care and labour to the author."[20] Eliot Singer observes of the murder mystery's foundational structure that "there [must] be an apparent crime (usually a murder), that someone seek to solve that crime, and that the reader not learn of the solution until the final epiphany"; he assesses Christie's accomplishments not primarily from a literary perspective but from a riddling one, determining that her success arose in her ability to devise "a satisfactory solution to a mystery," one that "must be acceptable as *rationally* superior to those alternatives that the reader has conceived."[21] As these viewpoints collectively evince, the narrative structure of mystery novels is simultaneously protean yet rigid, adaptable but conventional.

Cognizant of these challenging conditions, authors of mystery fiction face rather constrained possibilities for their endings, and it is again useful to contrast these strictures with the freedoms of literary fiction, in which a variety of endings can be imagined. *Jane Eyre* ends happily with Jane's marriage to Rochester, but it could end equally effectively if Jane left Rochester to pursue further her journey of self-discovery. Imagining Christie's novels with different killers, however, would require their plots to be reformulated in fundamental ways. (The exception to this general principle is evident in the theatrical adaptation of *Appointment with Death,* for which Christie exonerated the novel's killer and implicated a different character as the killer, with a different motive.) Moreover, the stringent limitations on the narrative structures of murder mysteries open an innovative manner for reading them, one by and large untransmittable to literary fiction: in reverse order. As one character explains to another in Christie's *The Burden,* some texts afford a variant path of reading that eschews the expected pattern of moving from beginning to end: "I take a look at the start, get some idea of what it's all about, then I go on to the end and see where the fellow has got to, and what he's been trying to prove. And then, *then* I go back and see *how* he's got there and what's made him land up where he did. Much more interesting" (55). Rather than consuming mystery novels in a linear fashion—in the terms of Gustav Freytag and his classic analysis of narrative structure, from the introduction (or exposition), to the rising action (or complication), to the climax, to the falling action (or return), and finally to the catastrophe (or dénouement)—some readers of mystery novels (including this author's maternal grandmother) commence with the introduction / exposition, turn to the catastrophe / dénouement, and then read the book for the pleasure of seeing the clues that they would likely have missed without first knowing the novel's conclusion.[22]

Regarding the plots of detective fiction, the simple requirement that a murder mystery include a murder severely constrains the author's creativity. The lion's share of most mystery novels details the investigation of the crime, and here too the author is challenged to maintain the reader's interest throughout passages depicting the detective interviewing the various suspects. Again, the basic structure of such a plot requires little extraneous information beyond dialogue and brief descriptions of settings that might provide clues, and so the author must, in effect, camouflage the simplicity of the structure by changing settings, introducing subplots, slipping in red herrings, and other such tactics. In a telling passage, Hastings indicates that interviews *qua* conversations dominate his recollection of events: "My narrative of the days spent at Styles must necessarily be somewhat rambling. In my recollection of it, it presents itself to me as a series of conversations—of suggestive words and phrases that etched themselves into my consciousness" (*Curtain*, 43). With Hastings's words Christie tacitly acknowledges the challenges of camouflaging conversations as narrative action, yet the conversations between the detective and the suspects occupy the narrative space between the crime and its resolution. Christie's unique ability as a writer is evident in her ability to keep the story progressing despite these limitations; as Ariadne Oliver states: "What really matters is plenty of *bodies*! If the thing's getting a little dull, some more blood cheers it up" (*Cards on the Table*, 51).

Along with the attacks on her style, characters, settings, and plots, another reason why Christie's murder mysteries have received such a critical drubbing emerges in the fact that her career largely coincides with the rise of modernist literature, which innovated new storytelling techniques, including stream-of-conscious narration, fragmented perspectives, and alienated protagonists. Resisting these tides, Christie preferred a more straightforward narrative style as represented by such writers she revered as Charles Dickens and Alexandre Dumas. She cited *Bleak House* as her favorite of Dickens's novels and detailed the period when "the works of Alexandre Dumas in French . . . entranced me" (*Autobiography* 137).[23] Christie's novels, with their linear plots told by third-person, and occasional first-person, narrators, appear uninterested in developing new narrative styles, yet Christie herself read widely in modernist literature. As Merja Makinen notes, *The Hollow* echoes key themes of Virginia Woolf's *To the Lighthouse,* primarily in their attention to women artists pursuing their visions,[24] and Nicholas Birns and Margaret Boe Birns align Christie's "theatrical procedures . . . with their emphasis on character" to "those of such modernist dramatists as Yeats, with his interest in 'masks,' or Brecht, who sees character as above all a way of highlighting social convention, radically foregrounding the characteristics of a given scene."[25] In recalling her reading history, Christie acknowledged her debts to the premier modernist poet T. S. Eliot, evident in the title of the Mary Westmacott novel *The Rose and the Yew Tree,* an allusion to his *Four Quartets:* "The moment of the rose and the moment of the yew-tree / Are of equal duration."[26]

In contrast to these modernist touches, at numerous points throughout her novels Christie obliquely indicates her lack of appreciation for innovative literary and artistic forms. Indeed, the character Raymond West, Miss Marple's nephew, offers little narrative purpose other than for Christie to satirize modern literary fiction, such as when she records his reaction to being mistaken for an author of popular fiction. "'I don't write detective stories,' said Raymond West, horrified at the mere idea" ("Greenshaw's Folly," *Double Sin,* 133), with his shock establishing the contrast between his literary ideals and the dross of genre fiction. Christie's narrators pointedly distinguish between literary success and financial success, as measured in the sales of West's books. "Although Raymond West was a 'big name' in literature, he could hardly be described as a best-seller. Though softening a bit with the advent of middle-age, his books dealt bleakly with the sordid side of life" ("Greenshaw's Folly," *Double Sin,* 120), the narrator declares, with a similar point made in *Sleeping Murder:* "Raymond West was a well-known (rather than popular) novelist" (11). Notwithstanding her nephew's opinions, Miss Marple frequently expresses her impatience with modernist fiction. In her typical self-effacing manner, she first disqualifies her opinion—"I know that in comparison with you young people I'm not clever at all"—but then delivers a withering denouncement of modernist fiction and art: "Raymond writes those very modern books all about rather unpleasant young men and women—and Joan paints those very remarkable pictures of square people with curious bulges on them" ("Miss Marple Tells a Story," *Regatta,* 111). In *Sleeping Murder,* Raymond West lauds the play *They Walked Without Feet* as "absolutely the most significant piece of drama for the last twenty years," but Gwenda's reaction indicates her preference for entertainment over edification, as the narrator reports that she "flinched slightly at the prospect of *They Walked Without Feet,* but supposed she might enjoy it—only the point about 'significant' plays was that you usually didn't" (16). Initially similar to Raymond West in his literary ambitions, Edmund Swettenham, the struggling novelist of *A Murder Is Announced,* describes his efforts in literary modernism: "I began writing a novel. Rather good it was. Pages about an unshaved man getting out of bed and what he smelt like, and the gray streets, and a horrible old woman with dropsy and a vicious young tart who dribbled down her chin—and they all talked interminably about the state of the world and wondered what they were alive for" (225). He renounces these efforts to write a farce, in the recognition that many readers desire entertainment over edification, in an apt echoing of Christie's career.

As much as Christie is most remembered for her detective fiction, her literary fiction—the six novels published under the *nom de plume* Mary Westmacott —allows for a deeper assessment of her talents, ambitions, and relationship to modernist literature. What is perhaps most striking about the Westmacott novels is their vastly differing narrative interests: the *künstlerroman* of musician Vernon Deyre in *Giant's Bread;* the thinly veiled autobiography of *Unfinished Portrait;* the searing psychological profile of a woman who realizes—and then chooses to forget—her personal failings in *Absent in the Spring;* the intersection of political and erotic intrigues in *The Rose and the Yew Tree;* the intergenerational struggles and rivalries of a mother and daughter in *A Daughter's a Daughter;* and the charged sibling dynamics of *The Burden.* Christie's Westmacott novels garnered high praise from several contemporary reviewers, evident in Orville Prescott's *New York Times* review of *Absent in the Spring,* which he calls a "mordantly clever story that is in some danger of being overlooked," observing that "Miss Westmacott strips her heroine of every shred of character and then finishes her brilliant satire with a stunning and absolutely inevitable climax."[27] The *New York Times* reviewer of *Unfinished Portrait* affirms that the novel "is worth reading for its sympathetic—and sometimes very amusing—account of [the protagonist's] childhood."[28] In her forays away from detective fiction into the realm of literary fiction, Christie demonstrated the artificiality of this divide, proving herself adept in both métiers.

If we accept the hypothesis that in many instances the division between genre fiction and literary fiction dissolves when assessing the great variety of fiction as a whole, it is nonetheless clear that this distinction remains of critical importance for marketing and selling books. That is to say, as a work of genre fiction may evince notable literary accomplishments, and as a work of literary fiction may engage deeply with the tropes of genre fiction, publishers market their books to maximize sales, which frequently involves pigeonholing them into recognizable genres. Obviously, Christie mostly wrote mystery novels; it is neither slander nor praise to state this fact and to observe these books were marketed as such. In complementary contrast, Christie's publishers sought to frame the Mary Westmacott novels, which lean more toward literary fiction than to genre fiction, as romances. Christie includes romance elements in many of her mystery novels, such as the courtship and marriage of Anne Beddingfield in *The Man in the Brown Suit* and of Tommy and Tuppence Beresford in *The Secret Adversary,* but she appeared impatient with the genre as a whole, evident in a satirical moment in *The Clocks* when the narrator comments on *Naked Love,* the newest manuscript of author Armand Levine: "Its painstaking eroticism left her uninterested—as indeed it did most of Mr. Levine's readers, in spite of his efforts. He was a notable example of the fact that nothing can be duller than dull pornography. In spite of lurid jackets and provocative titles, his sales went down every year" (2). As this brief incident indicates, Christie realized that longstanding generic tropes can deaden a romance novel if deployed overextensively. Situating the Westmacott novels as romances, Christie's publishers dubbed *The Burden* "a novel of romance and mystery," and on the back cover added, "Under the name of Mary Westmacott, Agatha Christie has also written *Absent in the Spring* and *A Daughter's a Daughter.* Her stories of romantic intrigue are among the finest in the genre."[29] The back cover of *A Daughter's a Daughter* praises it as a "suspenseful novel of love and passion," and *The Rose and the Yew Tree* is similarly lauded as a "probing and suspenseful novel that reveals the conflicting passions of two men—and the woman they both wanted." While these brief descriptions are true on a surface level, they camouflage Christie's forays in literary fiction under the rubric of romance, thus obscuring the extent of their deeper plots and the liberties she takes with this form.

Similar in style to her mystery fiction, Christie's Westmacott novels push their plots forward energetically with crisp dialogue and brevity of expression, as Christie refrains from excessive descriptions. As the narrator of *Unfinished Portrait* declares: "I'm not going into details—this isn't a chronicle of such things. There's no need to describe the quaint little Spanish town, or the meal we had together at her hotel, or the way I had my luggage secretly conveyed from my hotel to the one she was staying at" (21). From Christie's own perspective, *Absent in the Spring* represented the apex of her efforts: "Shortly after [*Death Comes as the End*], I wrote the one book [*Absent in the Spring*] that has satisfied me completely. It was a new Mary Westmacott, the book that I had always wanted to write, that had been clear in my mind. It was the picture of a woman with a complete image of herself, of what she was, but about which she was completely mistaken. Through her own actions, her own feelings and thoughts, this would be revealed to the reader" (*Autobiography*, 484). The novel ends with the protagonist's husband thinking of her, "You are alone and you always will be. But, please God, you'll never know it" (*Absent in the Spring,* 192). It is a brief and powerful ending, one that conveys the protagonist's limitations as a human being and her husband's devoted attention to protecting her from this knowledge. As Gillian Gill theorizes, through the Westmacott pseudonym, Christie divulged more of her personal experiences and viewpoints to her readers than in the works published under her name: "Through the elaborate self-masking device of Mary Westmacott, Agatha Christie felt free to speak to the reader more directly and openly than anywhere else. The woman who had hated to 'part with information' and who had changed herself into the Mistress of Mystery felt an imperative need for at least one outlet for the expression of her own personality, experience, ideas, and emotions."[30] Freed from the parameters of mystery fiction, the six Westmacott novels offer a wider view of Christie's talents, with many showcasing her skill with modernist techniques.

To identify Agatha Christie as a "Poet of Genre Fiction" is to recognize the paradox of her accomplishments, as she negotiated the requirements of genre fiction against a sea of reviewers who too often assessed her writing as if she were attempting to be the next Virginia Woolf. While cranking away as a "sausage factory," she penned novels that evince her ear for language, her recognition of the constraints of character, her judicious if minimal use of settings, and her attention to plots above virtually all other considerations. In this light, Christie's early forays into poetry were not a side path on the road to genre fiction, but an early and instructive period in her growth as an artist.

SIX

The Tragicomic Themes of Christie's Murders

"There is nothing immoral in my books—only murder," Agatha Christie once stated, in an amusingly ironic assessment of her fiction.[1] Murder victims, it can be safely assumed, would find the circumstances of their dispatch neither moral nor comic, and, in appraising their fates, surely they would agree that their untimely ends leaned more to the realm of tragedy than of farce. Yet in another key indicator of her talents, Christie aligns many of her mysteries with the humorous tradition of the comedy of manners, dissecting the foibles of polite society when murder—the ultimate disruption to a dinner party or other such social setting—ungraciously intrudes. Along with her titles as Queen of Crime of the Golden Age of Detective Fiction and Queen of the Cozies, Christie has been dubbed by Mary Jean DeMarr the "accepted mother of the comic village form," pointing to the prevalence of humorous moments in her small-town settings, notably Miss Marple's village of St. Mary Mead.[2] In a complementary fashion, Christie imbues several of her murders with a tragic cast, despite the claims of some critics that her novels lack emotional depth owing to their static characters and formulaic, if ingenious, plots. On the contrary, the demises of such victims as Linnet Ridgeway Doyle in *Death on the Nile,* Mrs. Boynton in *Appointment with Death,* and John Christos in *The Hollow* highlight her attention to the emotional causes and repercussions of murder, thereby refusing to allow her readers solely the pleasure of a puzzle and imbuing her novels with a philosophical weight as she ponders the consequences of lives untimely ended. As Christie's steady engagement with the protocols of detective fiction illustrate her expansive exploitation of the possibilities of the form, her engagement with tropes of comedy and tragedy similarly evinces her deployment of literary and theatrical traditions to elevate her themes.

Comedy and tragedy are rooted in, although not constrained by, theatrical traditions, and, congruent with her status as a preeminent playwright of the twentieth century, Christie clearly envisioned many of her murders and plots theatrically. In adapting several of her novels into plays, including *And Then There Were None, Death on the Nile* (as *Hidden Horizon*), *Appointment with Death,* and *Towards Zero,* among others, Christie navigated the different effects of these forms, striving to simplify the complexity of her plots and to enhance their dramatic appeal. More so, throughout her novels murders assume a dramatic and theatrical tenor. In *The Hollow* the murder appears staged, as the narrator reports: "For what [Poirot] was looking at was a highly artificial murder scene," including an "artistically arranged" body (83). Commenting on a character's timely entrance, Poirot states delightedly, "My dear Mr. Schwartz, you appeared in the nick of time. It might have been a drama on the stage!" ("The Erymanthian Boar," *Labors of Hercules,* 75). *Mrs. McGinty's Dead* features "pre-eminently a theatrical murder" (206), and the killer, Robin Upward, is a playwright. "One gets in the habit, you know, of looking at things from the point of view of a stage set, rather than from the point of view of reality," a character asserts in *Murder with Mirrors* (151), with these words hinting at the blurring of narrative "reality" with Christie's sense of theatricality.

In overarching terms, comedy and tragedy can be distinguished by their emphases on life and death: for the most part, comedies end in community harmony, often signaled by marriage and thus the promise of the future reproduction of this newly reunited community.[3] In contrast, tragedies typically conclude in deaths representing the fragmentation of the social order. Murder mysteries cannot be easily transposed onto these schemata: they invert the standard tragic plot by opening, not concluding, with deaths, as they also frequently eschew the humor upon which comedy depends, even if their dénouements might feature the restitution of community harmony and the promised union of a romantic couple. Despite these potential imbalances in tone and scope, Christie infuses her murders with comic and tragic tropes, lightening some with levity, deepening others with gravitas, while elevating the genre as a whole.

The Comedy of Christie's Murders

In the virtual self-satire of "The Mystery of the Spanish Shawl," it is evident that Christie assumed an ultimately comic view on the challenges of writing detective fiction. This short story opens by detailing the travails of Mr. Eastwood, a struggling neophyte novelist, and it is difficult not to see Christie herself in this somewhat exaggerated scene, as surely she found herself occasionally perplexed concerning how to develop one of her initial ideas into a fully formed novel: "'THE MYSTERY OF THE SECOND CUCUMBER,' so it ran. A pleasing title. Anthony

Eastwood felt that anyone reading that title would be at once intrigued and arrested by it. 'The Mystery of the Second Cucumber,' they would say. 'What can that be about? A cucumber? The second cucumber? I must certainly read that story.' And they would be thrilled and charmed by the consummate ease with which this master of detective fiction had woven an exciting plot round this simple vegetable" ("The Mystery of the Spanish Shawl," *Witness for the Prosecution*, 139). Here Christie finds humor in the writer's common frustration of what precisely she is going to write, which suggests her attention to the latent humor of vexing circumstances. Anthony Eastwood's second cucumber thus metonymically represents the likely disjunction between murder and humor but also their surprising union in Christie's hands, and it is precisely owing to the ugliness of murder that Christie's humor shines through in their glaring yet productive contrast.

"Of course, say what you like, a murder *is* an awkward thing—it upsets the servants and puts the general routine out," proclaims Lady Angkatell in *The Hollow* (90), to which the reader is seemingly solicited to nod in sympathy, *Ah, yes, the ordeals that plague the wealthy in Christie's England, from the distressed domestic to the occasional murder!* Lady Angkatell's words also apparently indicate that murders occur with relative frequency among the rarefied realms of Britain's elite, as if this aggrieved, if not quite distressed, hostess has experienced such turmoils repeatedly. At the very least, Lady Angkatell considers the worrisome implications of pursuing one's social life during the aftermath of a murder, as she explains the etiquette of consuming dessert amidst such untimely circumstances: "There would be something very gross, just after the death of a friend, in eating one's favourite pudding. But caramel custard is so easy . . . and then one leaves a little on one's plate" (*Hollow*, 100). To eat one's favorite pudding after a murder would shockingly abrogate the manners of polite society, but no one could object to a caramel custard, particularly if the diners leave behind a lonesome morsel to indicate their mourning, which is not to imply that they are actually experiencing sorrow. *The Hollow* stands as one of Christie's most entertaining and ingenious novels for several reasons—notably the solution to the murder which is simultaneously extraordinarily clever but rather simple—but also in its religious themes, as the murder of Dr. John Christow becomes an allegory of the killer's loss of faith. As evident from Lady Angkatell's observations on the social proprieties of murder, the novel also triumphs in its steady attention to comic themes, and thus exemplifies a prevailing thread throughout much of Christie's fiction: her frequent interweaving of the humor of a comedy of manners into a murder mystery, resulting in novels as amusing as they are perplexing. To some degree Christie's interest in the comedy of manners tradition should not be surprising: her first effort at novel writing, *Snow upon the Desert*, is a comedy of manners, which testifies to her early interest in satirizing the foibles of English society.[4] Indeed, Marty Knepper identifies *Murder at the Vicarage,* Miss Marple's debut novel, as "a marvelous comedy of manners."[5]

The comedy of manners establishes a sense of decorum, only for the characters then to flaunt these rules of decorum. David Hirst explains this theatrical genre: "The subject of the comedy of manners is the way people behave, the manners they employ in a social context; the chief concerns of the characters are sex and money (and the interrelated topics of marriage, adultery and divorce); the style is distinguished by the refinement of raw emotional expression in the subtlety of wit and intrigue."[6] Shakespeare's *Much Ado about Nothing* is often celebrated as the first comedy of manners in English theatre, and famed playwrights of this tradition include William Congreve (*The Way of the World*), Richard Brinsley Sheridan (*The Rivals*), and Oscar Wilde (*The Importance of Being Earnest*). Murder mysteries and comedies of manners potentially overlap in their joint interest in their characters' mercenary and amorous motivations, as well as the ways that these motivations disrupt the surrounding community. Hirst further states that "the keynote of these plays is decorum. This has given rise to another criticism: that of a shallowness and lack of sincerity in the characters and their authors."[7] As discussed in the previous chapter, the alleged shallowness of Christie's characters mostly arises from the fact that their emotional development must occur before the novel's inciting event of murder, and thus before much of its narrative action, but any such shallowness can also reflect their participation in the human comedy of life in a cloistered society. Certainly, Miss Marple knows the strictures of etiquette and decorum and refuses to break them, such as when she reacts to surprising circumstances by not reacting: "True to the precepts handed down to her by her mother and grandmother—to wit: that a true lady can neither be shocked nor surprised—Miss Marple merely raised her eyebrows" (*What Mrs. McGillicuddy Saw!* 8).

As much as *The Hollow* could be classified as a murder mystery influenced by the comedy of manners tradition, Christie's theatrical version of *The Hollow* could be inversely classified as a comedy of manners influenced by the traditions of detective fiction. Consider Lady Angkatell's response to her husband's subtle suggestion that she might be the culprit: "Darling, darling, you don't imagine for a moment that *I* shot John? (*She laughs, rises, crosses to the fireplace and picks up the box of chocolates from the mantelpiece.*) I did have that silly idea about an accident. But then I remembered that he was our guest. . . . One doesn't ask someone to be a guest and then get behind a bush and have a pop at them" (*TMAOP,* 243). These lines join together a variety of comic tropes: Lady Angkatell's languid repetition of "darling," her airy laughter, her appetite for chocolates during what should be a serious discussion, her light confession that she had indeed considered dispatching the victim, and finally her capitulation to the demands of etiquette that one should not murder one's guests. She soon adds, "What a pity John Cristow's dead. Really quite unnecessary after all. But what an exciting weekend" (*TMAOP*, 248). In one of her final lines, she sighs winsomely, "It was a wonderful inquest" (*TMAOP*, 260). Many comedies contrast their outré and excessive characters with so-called "straight men," and it is evident that Christie envisioned this play's detective, Inspector Colqhuhoun, as filling this role: "*a thoughtful quiet man with charm and a sense of humour. His personality is sympathetic. He must not be played as a comedy part*" (*TMAOP*, 210). Notably, Christie replaced Hercule Poirot with Inspector Colqhuhoun for her stage adaptation of *The Hollow*, thus to deflate the audience's expectation that Poirot fill a comic role in this instance, as he frequently does in her novels owing to his sardonic view of English culture.

Christie's comic stylings can be productively aligned to Oscar Wilde's, as several of her characters reflect types common to the comedy of manners tradition as exemplified by his masterpiece, *The Importance of Being Earnest*. The artist Cedric Crackenthorpe channels Wilde's Algernon Moncrieff when he claims, "Of course I despise money when I haven't got any. . . . It's the only dignified thing to do" (*What Mrs. McGillicuddy Saw!* 190), and readers hear an echo of Wilde's imperiously aloof Lady Bracknell in Christie's treatment of Miss Hartnell, one of Miss Marple's neighbors: "She visited the poor indefatigably, however hard they tried to avoid her ministrations" (*Body in the Library*, 36). Comedies of manners often treat romantic and even adulterous affairs in a mock scandalous manner, evident when Clarissa, a married woman, asks, "Are you making immoral advances to me, Jeremy?" He candidly replies, "Definitely," and she acquiesces immediately to her ostensible debauchment: "How lovely. Go on" (*Spider's Web*, 13). Within comic scenarios, domestics such as Mrs. Kidder often aspire to break the bonds of decorum by gossiping about their employers, as illustrated in her conversation with the imperturbable Lucy Eyelesbarrow: "'Dreadful, the things people go about saying. I don't listen, mind you, more than I can help. But you'd hardly believe it.' She waited hopefully" (*What Mrs. McGillicuddy Saw!* 194). One should be able to trust the authority and competency of the police, but when Chief Inspector Davy, shaking "his head gently and reassuringly," comforts Miss Marple that the mysterious events at Bertram's Hotel will not continue—"There won't be any murders" (*At Bertram's Hotel*, 143)—he is proved incompetent and incorrect in the very next sentences when another murder occurs: "A sharp report, louder than the former one, came from outside. It was followed by a scream and another report" (144). Comedies often rely on mistaken identities, such as when snobbish Mrs. Schuyler is horrified that "the outrageous Mr. Ferguson" is courting her cousin Cornelia—"Cornelia . . . *have you encouraged this young man?*"—only to quickly change her opinion when Poirot informs her that Ferguson's true identity is the "young Lord Dawlish. Rolling in money, of course" (*Death on the Nile*, 217–18). Comedy, in many ways, consists of the art of inverting and reversing expectations, which these brief scenes aptly illustrate.

Despite the discovery of a murder victim, the opening scenes of *The Body in the Library* further illuminate Christie's treatment of murder as a comedy of manners. As Neil McDonald observes, Christie relies on "more than a touch of comedy in the ways she deployed her outrageous plots,"[8] which is readily evident as Mrs. Bantry wakes from her dreams of winning first prize at a flower show, which also featured the vicar's wife in her bathing suit, to the hysterical cries of Mary, her maid: "Oh, ma'am, oh, ma'am, there's a body in the library" (2). Mrs. Bantry and her husband bicker amicably over the unlikeliness of this reported corpse and then confirm its presence. The social disruption caused by murder escalates improprieties of etiquette, as Miss Marple is surprised to receive a phone call before the accustomed hour of nine in the morning. Mrs. Bantry oddly and volubly compliments Miss Marple. "You're so good at bodies," she effuses, and soon adds, "you're very good at murders" (7). Mrs. Bantry then explains her plan to amuse herself despite this misfortune: "What I feel is that if one has got to have a murder actually happening in one's house, one might as well enjoy it, if you know what I mean" (8). The scene concludes as Mrs. Bantry notes a point of disagreement with her husband: "He seems to think I shouldn't enjoy myself about it at all" (8). Mrs. Bantry perceives murder as an amusing interruption of life's quotidian fare, whereas Mr. Bantry rejects any pleasures afforded by crime and instead insists that they present a façade of concern—in effect, revealing their joint comic duplicity, if for separate purposes.

Without the feelings of the victims to consider, the suspects and survivors find themselves in an array of socially awkward situations, particularly with the bleak yet ironic realization that "anyone's safety depends principally on the fact that nobody wishes to kill them" (*Easy to Kill*, 173). Indeed, even murder victims are at times treated as breaching social etiquette due to the indignity of their untimely demises. In *Cat among the Pigeons*, the newspapers, in reporting the death of a school teacher, "had an almost apologetic note in [their reports], as though it were thoroughly tactless of any games mistress to get herself shot in such circumstances" (85). In comedies of manners, characters often deliver their lines in a deadpan style—what they say is funny, but they do not acknowledge its humor—and this paradigm enlivens Christie's characterization of Poirot. She emphasizes his determined pursuit of justice for murder victims, yet she embellishes his personality through his droll replies to others. When Colonel Race reacts exasperatedly to the theatrical, alcoholic, and erratic Mrs. Otterbourne— "What a poisonous woman! Whew! Why didn't somebody murder *her*?"— Poirot calms his friend: "'It may yet happen,' Poirot consoled him" (*Death on the Nile*, 159). When two teen boys spin out increasingly farfetched scenarios to explain a murder, the narrator records their eager anticipation of Poirot's approval—"They both looked with satisfied faces to Poirot"—but his response records the disjunction between their viewpoints: "Well . . . you've certainly given me something to think about" (*Hallowe'en Party*, 143). In another such exchange, Mrs. Clapperton wonders aloud, "But really, M. Poirot, what would one *be* if one wasn't alive?" to which Poirot succinctly replies, "Dead." Christie then details his interlocutor's reaction: "Mrs. Clapperton frowned. The reply was not to her liking. The man, she decided, was trying to be funny" ("Problem at Sea," *Regatta,* 171).

Miss Marple generates similar reactions, such as when she explains the intricacies of a murder and another character shudders, "That old lady gives me the creeps" (*Nemesis,* 223). Miss Marple's insistence on propriety also gives rise to humorous euphemisms, evident when readers learn of her distaste for the word *nymphomania:* "Indeed it was not a word that Miss Marple would have used—her own phrase would have been 'always too fond of men'" (*At Bertram's Hotel,* 15). The wit of many comedies of manners hinges on an epigrammatic style, evident in Wilde's razor-sharp quips; Christie's wit is often epigrammatic, as in her definition of a "real Conservative" as one who "preferred acute boredom to the meretriciously amusing" (*The Rose and the Yew Tree,* 37). When one of Christie's characters opines sardonically, "If you can't have a gentleman, I suppose a hero is the next best thing," the narrator assesses these words as "practically an epigram" (38).

Many of Christie's characters also display comic foibles in their characterizations, as she applies deftly comic and individualizing touches that leaven their supporting roles in the unfolding plots. Poirot's secretary Miss Lemon could be excised from the novels altogether with little loss to their storylines, yet her monomaniacal obsession with her filing system elevates a forgettable figure into a memorable one: "Her real passion in life was the perfection of a filing system beside which all other filing systems should sink into oblivion. She dreamed of such a system at night" ("How Does Your Garden Grow?" *Regatta,* 47). *Hickory Dickory Death* opens with Poirot incredulous at Miss Lemon's three typing errors, with the social fabric of his household upset by this intrusion of disorder. As the narrator explains: "It was well known that the whole of Miss Lemon's heart and mind was given, when she was not on duty, to the perfection of a new filing system which was to be patented and bear her name" (2). All told, Miss Lemon emerges as a strikingly unique comic character: one who would never see herself as such, owing to her strict professionalism, but one who appears as such to readers precisely because of the excesses of this professionalism.

Truly, Christie often takes an unabashedly optimistic view of murder in her novels, in which untimely deaths are not to be unduly lamented but appreciated as part of life's rhythms. Jerry Burton, the first-person narrator of *The Moving Finger,* takes comfort in his valedictory evaluation of life's ephemerality, despite the murderous circumstances prompting these thoughts: "Just for a fleeting moment I thought of Mrs. Symmington and Agnes Woddell in their graves in the churchyard and wondered if they would agree, and then I remembered that Agnes' boyfriend hadn't been very fond of her and that Mrs. Symmington hadn't been very nice to Megan, and what the hell? We've all got to die sometime! And I agreed with Miss Emily that everything was for the best in the best of possible worlds" (180). A rosier view of murder could hardly be envisioned: the inevitability of death awaits us one and all, and so death cannot help but be appreciated as an unavoidable experience in life, as part of "the best of possible worlds" that facilitates human existence (even if we have no choice in the matter). The disparate fortunes of life and death are often noted in passing fashion, in lines that could be read either mournfully or mordantly, with the latter interpretation illuminating Christie's insights into the latent humor of death. Such a dual interpretation is also evident in the successful efforts of Mrs. Spenlow, formerly a between-maid but now a shopkeeper, to raise her financial prospects: "The shop had prospered. Not so [her husband], who before long had sickened and died" ("Tape-Measure Murder," *Three Blind Mice*, 93). Tears over Mr. Spenlow's untimely passing, it appears, would merely be wasted.

Finally, it should be stressed that the line between comedy and tragedy can be surprisingly thin, as evident in the following exchange from *Remembered Death*, which commences in a comedy-of-manners style. Lord Kidderminster believes that one's duty to the common good requires him to report any homicidal infractions committed by his family members and is shocked by Lady Kidderminster's suggestion that he should withhold any such information: "If my daughter's a murderess, do you suggest that I should use my official position to rescue her from the consequences of her act?" Lady Kidderminster tersely replies, "Of course." Lord Kidderminster reiterates his viewpoint—"My dear Vicky! You don't understand! One can't do things like that. It would be a breach of—of honour." She again dismisses his ethical stance: "Rubbish." Such a comic pairing of earnestness and insouciance injects a note of humor in the scene, but then Christie sharply changes its tone: "They looked at each other—so far divided that neither could see the other's point of view. So might Agamemnon and Clytemnestra have stared at each other with the word Iphigenia on their lips" (*Remembered Death*, 144). With this reference to one of the more dysfunctional of families from Greek legends, as Agamemnon sacrifices their daughter Iphigenia for propitious winds to sail to Troy, for which Clytemnestra and her lover Aegisthus murder him on his return, the reader may well wonder if similar fates might befall these characters, particularly as Christie occasionally uses well-known tragedies to signal and foreshadow her plots. This succinct scene between the Kidderminsters captures the ephemerality of a particularly charged and potentially momentous conversation—from the humor of discordant social and familial views to the latent chance that their differences might result in one or the other's murder. In another such moment, Hercule Poirot observes of a murder victim, "Yes, she is dead. . . . Someone has turned the comedy into a tragedy" ("The Theft of the Royal Ruby," *Double Sin,* 75), and then tragedy again metamorphoses into comedy when it turns out that the victim, Bridget, is not really dead after all. Christie again comments on the tenuous line between comedy and tragedy in a moment from *The Rose and the Yew,* when a character discusses Shakespeare's *Othello* and, in commenting on Iago, identifies him as the tragic counterweight of the playwright's great comic figure, Falstaff: "Falstaff stuff, only this time it's not comedy but tragedy" (*The Rose and the Yew Tree,* 140). For Christie, tragedy is not the flipside of the comedy but its potential continuity.

Christie's Tragedies

At their core, tragedies focus on the human body in suffering and agony, as their protagonists fall to their personal failings and end in misery and death. According to Aristotelian dramatic theory, the conclusion of a tragedy is intended to incite a cathartic reaction from the audience, and the conclusions of mystery novels can function similarly, as readers experience the revelation of the killer and the presumed restoration of civic order. In his rich account of the tragic tradition and in a formulation relevant to Christie's novels, Terry Eagleton writes: "Tragedy, then strikes a balance between meaning and mystery."[9] Tragedies ask haunting questions concerning the purpose of life and the finality of death that remain unanswerable, only ponderable, whereas murder mysteries touch upon these unanswerable questions while resolving the one at the heart of the novel, of who killed the victim and for what reason. "Murder is a drama. The desire for drama is very strong in the human race" (*Murder in Retrospect,* 79), opines Hercule Poirot, and murder mysteries align closely with tragedies in their joint focus on the painful condition of the human body and the loss of life. In this light, many murder mysteries can be seen as tragedies with solutions.

A pall of tragedy hangs over many of Christie's novels, a theme keenly evident in the opening pages of *Ordeal by Innocence.* Arthur Calgary, returning from an Antarctic expedition that precluded him from testifying and proving the innocence of a wrongly convicted man, begins his quest for atonement by confronting the implacability of fate: "To his already overstimulated imagination, it seemed as though Tragedy herself stood there barring his way. It was a young face; indeed, it was in the poignancy of its youth that tragedy had its very essence. The Tragic Mask, he thought, should always be a mask of youth. . . . Helpless, foreordained, with a doom approaching . . . from the future" (*Ordeal by Innocence,* 5). Fate bears inexorably down upon tragic protagonists, who cannot escape their destinies but must proceed apace to the disastrous climax.

As Susanne Langer notes: "The mythical tradition of Greece treated the fate of its 'heroes' . . . as a mysterious power inherent in the world rather than in the man and his ancestry; it was conceived as a private incubus bestowed on him at birth by a vengeful deity."[10] Arthur Calgary sees himself as similarly afflicted, as he muses: "The tragedy that ended his life has darkened my own" (*Ordeal by Innocence*, 19). Such are the destinies awaiting so many of Christie's characters, notably the murder victims but also sundry others ensnared in the killer's (and the author's) plots.

As many critics have observed, several of Shakespeare's great tragedies—notably *Hamlet, Macbeth,* and *Othello*—can be read as murder mysteries themselves, but if not precisely as "whodunnits" than as "whydunnits," in which the playwright explores the affective motivations that result in carnage and carcasses on stage. Shakespeare's influence on Christie is evident in a range of her novels, but as Christie likely tired of critics unfavorably comparing her to literary authors, Hercule Poirot, in an additional example of his forays in literary criticism, pinpoints Shakespeare's faults as a mystery writer:

> Iago is the perfect murderer. The deaths of Desdemona, of Cassio—even of Othello himself—are all Iago's crimes, planned by him, carried out by him. And he remains outside the circle, untouched by suspicion—or could have done so. For your great Shakespeare, my friend, had to deal with the dilemma that his own art had brought about. To unmask Iago, he had to resort to the clumsiest of devices—the handkerchief—a piece of work not at all in keeping with Iago's general technique and a blunder of which one feels certain he would not have been guilty. (*Curtain*, 167)

Despite this pointed slight at Shakespeare's plotting skills, Christie found inspiration in a range of his tragedies, thus to deepen her themes and the emotional impact of her murders. In a very real sense, both tragedies and murders result from mismanaged and untamed emotions, evident when Poirot discerns a Shakespearean undercast to the mysteries he is called to solve: "it is very Shakespearean—there are here all the emotions—the human emotions—in which Shakespeare would have revelled—the jealousies, the hates—the swift passionate actions" (*There Is a Tide,* 193).

Among the motivations of her murderers, a misguided or overzealous love ranks among the most common, which allows Christie to probe the complexity of human relationships in an inherently fallen world while playing murderous variations on a *Romeo and Juliet* theme. *Death on the Nile* illustrates these precepts in Jacqueline de Bellefort's realization that her love for Simon Doyle transformed her into a murderer, as the narrator reports: "She herself had not coveted Linnet Ridgeway's money, but she had loved Simon Doyle, had loved him beyond reason and beyond rectitude and beyond pity" (256). Upon learning the motivations behind the murders, another character states mournfully, "Love can be a very frightening thing," as Poirot then identifies the tragic cast to love: "That is why most great love stories are tragedies" (261–62). Ondřej Beran assesses the morality of Jacqueline's love for Simon and concludes that "she acts out of loyalty: to act otherwise would be difficult or impossible to reconcile with her love for Simon"; in other words, to do so "would be incompatible with who she is," and thus Christie ponders the very meaning of the self in relation to one's beloved.[11] In line with Beran's interpretation, readers are asked to contemplate the ways in which love shifts identities in potentially unwelcome ways. *Murder in Retrospect* envisions Elsa Greer as a Juliet figure driven to murder following the anguishing loss of her Romeo, an ending that the narrator foreshadows in an appraisal of her: "No Juliet here—unless perhaps one could imagine Juliet a survivor—living on, deprived of Romeo. Was it not an essential part of Juliet's make-up that she should die young?" (80). Christie imbues this narrative with a deeper tragic cast in Elsa's eventual realization that the ultimate victim of her murder was herself: "I didn't understand that I was killing *myself*—not him. . . . *I* died" (185).

From Poirot's perspective, the tragedy always potential in love extends across one's life, entrapping both the young and the old: "A tragedy of love may not always belong to Romeo and Juliet. It is not necessarily only the young who suffer the pains of love and are ready to die for love" (*Elephants Can Remember*, 186). More so, some characters, such as Victoria Jones in *They Came to Baghdad*, view *Romeo and Juliet* as a template through which to structure their lives, evident when she muses over her meeting and departure from handsome Edward: "She and Edward, she felt, were somewhat in the position of that unhappy couple, although perhaps Romeo and Juliet had expressed their feelings in rather more high class language" (17). Victoria persists in inhabiting the narrative position of Juliet virtually to the novel's conclusion, seeing herself "once more in the role of a modern Juliet, waiting for Romeo" (186). *They Came to Baghdad* admits a rosier ending than many of Christie's novels, as Victoria escapes an untimely demise by refusing the tragic conclusion meted out to Juliet and piercing through the veil of romanticism: "And as she looked at that beautiful evil face, all her silly adolescent calf love faded away, and she knew that what she felt for Edward had never been love. It had been the same feeling that she had experienced some years earlier for Humphrey Bogart, and later for the Duke of Edinburgh" (189). Soon after, she realizes, "I just had a thoroughly school-girl crush on him—fancying myself Juliet and all sorts of silly things" (216). Victoria Jones avoids the tragic fates of Jacqueline de Bellefort and Elsa Greer by refusing to metamorphose into a murderer, yet the novel similarly ponders the actions, even the possible atrocities, committed in the name of love.

Shakespeare's *Othello* likewise inspired a range of Christie's more tragically themed murders, evident in Poirot's analysis of Desdemona's demise: "The character of the victim has always something to do with his or her murder. The frank and unsuspicious mind of Desdemona was the direct cause of her death. A more suspicious woman would have seen Iago's machinations and circumvented them much earlier" (*Holiday for Murder*, 94). More than simply "victim blaming," Poirot's meditations on Desdemona detail the intimate connection between so many murderers and their victims, not for the purpose of glorifying an ultimately misbegotten affection but to highlight the impossibility of knowing the motives of even the people most beloved in our lives. Expanding this theme in *Endless Night*, Christie's first-person narrator Michael Rogers dismisses the possibility of fairy-tale endings, foreseeing the tragic events forthcoming: "'And so they got married and lived happily ever afterward.' You can't, after all, make a big drama out of living happily ever afterward" (53). Here Christie acknowledges a simple narrative truth—fairy tales end at the moment of "they lived happily ever after" because most narratives are based on conflict, not contentment—but this point holds exponentially true for murder mysteries. Furthermore, she builds the tragic cast inherent in narratives based on conflict when, ironically, Michael's wife Ellie foreshadows her own death by likening herself to Desdemona: "So I suppose I'd have had to be like Desdemona and deceived my father and run away with you" (131). Shakespeare's vision of love in *Othello*, in the possibility that one might be killed by one's beloved, is terrifyingly dark, and it heightens the emotional resonance of the many instances in which spouses murder their mates in Christie's fiction.

Besides the killers and their victims, the tragic force of Christie's murders ensnares a range of other characters in their aftermath. In a particularly striking instance of these dynamics, Mrs. Folliatt is forced to confront the horror of her son's wickedness: "I have always known. . . . Even as a child he frightened me. . . . Ruthless . . . without pity . . . and without conscience. . . . but he was my son and I loved him" (*Dead Man's Folly*, 180–81). A mother witnesses her son's depravities yet can do little to stop them and then must confront her own complicity in his evil. In an inversion of these tragic dynamics, the Boynton family, following the murder of their imperiously cruel stepmother, is rejuvenated by her death, in a conclusion that unsettlingly ponders the possible benefits of murder, that asks readers whether an untimely death should always be regretted. *Hallowe'en Party* features a modern-day Agamemnon in the character of Michael Garfield, who plans to murder his daughter in pursuit of his art: "Iphigenia. Agamemnon sacrificed his daughter so that he should get a wind to take his ships to Troy. Michael would have sacrificed his daughter so that he should have a new Garden of Eden" (215). With these and other families more murderous than nurturing,

Christie questions the foundations of human life and community, uncovering primal passions that demand the sacrifice of another.

As Christie employs tragic traditions to elevate the themes of her novels, she also cagily weaves them into her narratives as clues to the killer's motivations and as red herrings designed to deceive knowing readers into undue suspicion against innocent characters. As Lisa Hopkins argues of authors' use of allusions in detective fiction, "Shakespearean allusion also has consequences for the reader and for the status of the text itself: it interpellates the reader and establishes the literary status of the text."[12] Readers perceiving allusions to Shakespeare and other authors must disentangle these threads, piecing together the author's purpose in the reference and how it affects an understanding of the characters' motivations. For example, in *Remembered Death,* George Barton sees himself in Othello upon learning of his wife Rosemary's infidelity—"He understood in that moment just what Othello had felt" (66–67)—although when another character reminds him of her duplicity, he claims he was prepared for this betrayal (66–67). Another character admits his infatuation over Rosemary in Shakespearean terms—"Even Romeo . . . had his Rosaline before he was bowled over for good and all by Juliet" (102). Yet neither of these allusions provides insight into the objectives behind Rosemary's murder, which was committed for pecuniary motives unrelated to these Shakespearean echoes.

By interweaving comic and tragic elements in her mysteries, Christie unsettles readers' expectations before they open the pages of one of her novels. Will she find inspiration from her comic muse, as in *The Murder at the Vicarage, The Body in the Library,* and *The Hollow;* or from her tragic muse, as in *Ordeal by Innocence, Endless Night, Sleeping Murder;* or from both simultaneously, as in *Death on the Nile* and *Cat among the Pigeons*? Readers will only know once they open a novel's pages, for in addition to the identity of the killer, Christie's subgenres must be identified as well, with additional reading pleasures available from her polyvocal forms. Surely there is nothing tragic about that.

SEVEN

The Queer Insularity of Christie's England

In a strikingly candid assessment of her cloistered perspective on the world, Agatha Christie admitted: "I could never manage miners talking in pubs because I don't know what miners talk about in pubs."[1] The old adage that authors should write what they know holds true and false throughout the field of fiction, for any flights of fancy in which authors indulge while imagining new situations, new characters, and new plots must be counterbalanced by creating a general verisimilitude to their stories. Christie need not have personally experienced a murder occurring within her circle of acquaintances because her imagination compensated for this lack; in contrast, the settings depicted in her novels represent an English world of relative wealth and comfort that resembles the one in which she grew up and lived. Such a narrow perspective would apparently endorse a conservative vision of England, and, as Laura Thompson states in her biography of the author, "Agatha herself was a Conservative voter."[2] Aligned with this political conservatism, Christie upholds a traditional, conventional vision of England and its citizenry, evident in the simple fact that, spanning the decades during which she wrote her mysteries, the stately manor homes and close-knit rural villages remain overwhelmingly populated by white, straight, and financially comfortable characters.

Against this mostly uniform and mostly unquestioned cultural background, Christie simultaneously observes England's internal inconsistencies and prejudices, exposing the nation to a thorough critique. From these converging viewpoints, England is both historically conservative yet gradually liberalizing, both regressively retrograde in its views of races and ethnicities outside of white Anglo-Saxonism yet held up to scrutiny for its hidebound mores. Michael Moon proposes that Christie engages provocatively with cultural norms, demonstrating that, rather than monolithic phenomena, they are "playful, unpredictable, highly mobile, curious, omnivorous, generous in according value and attention —in several of the broader senses of the term, queer."[3] J. C. Bernthal sounds a similar note: "A premise that Christie self-consciously presented her characters as stereotypes has evolved into a realization that, in these texts, normality is presented as insecure, paranoid, frail, and theatrical. Normativity requires a set of pinpointed queers to define itself against."[4] *Queer*, in these instances and throughout this chapter, refers not exclusively to erotic desires and identities that undermine England's prevailing presumptions of heteronormativity but to a wider range of such subversions, including when characters subvert hitherto unquestioned ideals of Englishness. Such queer instances of her fiction destabilize the staid, conservative, and insular Englishness otherwise on display. On the whole, Christie's fiction reflects a queer sense of the nation's insularity, one in which norms are upheld and travestied, unquestioned yet surprisingly malleable.

But what is conservatism for a writer, and how does one recognize it in her novels? To take one example relevant to Christie's fictions, politically conservative viewpoints have long endorsed the death penalty, a perspective promulgated by Miss Marple when she states: "I am really very, very glad . . . that they haven't abolished capital punishment yet because I do feel that if there is anyone who ought to hang . . ." as she then identifies the culprit of *What Mrs. McGillicuddy Saw!* (228). Many strains of conservatism endorse traditional gender roles and condemn feminism, and *There Is a Tide . . .* offers a rather horrifically anti-feminist lesson when a woman reunites with her fiancé after he attempted to kill her: "When you caught hold of me by the throat and said if I wasn't for you, no one should have me—well—I knew then that I was your woman!" (213). Lamenting the social revolution of the 1960s and the freedoms it brought, the narrator of *Endless Night* realizes that he knows little of love, thereby echoing conservative diatribes on shifting sexual mores: "I didn't know at that time anything about love. All I knew about was sex. That was all anybody of my generation seemed to know about. We talked about it too much, I think, and heard too much about it and took it too seriously. We didn't know—any of my friends or myself—what it was really going to be when it happened. Love, I mean" (20). In a related example of these dynamics, does one perceive Christie's views of religion in her short story "Promotion in the Highest," which includes a jibe at Catholicism when St. Peter says: "I'm not so sure about that Church I founded. . . . It's not turned out at all as we meant" (*Star over Bethlehem* 57)? Anti-Catholic prejudice also appears in *Crooked House* when a character theorizes on the murderer's identity: "if it wasn't the Communists, mark my word, it was the Catholics. The Scarlet Woman of Babylon, that's what they are" (116). Similarly, characters occasionally express anti-Semitic perspectives, as illustrated when Mahmoud, the "stout dragoman" in *Appointment with Death*, cries, "My life all one misery! Ah! what with miseries and iniquities Jews do to us—" (140); another character later assesses, "That man's just crazy on the subject of the Jews. I don't think he's quite sane on the point" (161). Such viewpoints are expressed by Christie's characters, not by Christie herself, and so any attempt to discern her personal views from her fiction must disentangle them from her characters' words, personalities, and motivations; must assess her efforts to build her themes, particularly comic and ironic ones; and must grapple with the likelihood that her conservative views shifted, even if only partially, during the fifty-six years separating her first and last novels.

In a complementary tactic that challenges readers attempting to glean her viewpoints from her fiction, Christie often avoids taking sides in political debates. In several instances two characters represent opposing sides of a controversial topic, but she employs this technique to enhance their characterizations without committing herself to either perspective. *The Hollow,* published in 1946, features the comically imperious Lady Angkatell wryly baiting her interlocutor about taxation and social programs, with her words hinting at her conservative views: "I must have a talk with you, David, and learn all the new ideas. As far as I can see, one must hate everybody but at the same time give them free medical attention and a lot of extra education, poor things!" (111). Her words concerning "free medical attention" allude to contemporary debates concerning the National Health Service, which was established through general taxation in 1948 and has long been described as Great Britain's gift to its citizenry following the hardships of World War II. Both Lady Angkatell and David Angkatell are exaggerated characters—her gentility is excessive, as is his revolutionary fervor—and so readers are not encouraged to align themselves with either viewpoint.

In a particularly dazzling display of political neutrality, Christie describes a character who joins the Labour Party for motives of personal advancement rather than of ethical conviction: "Though by predilection a Liberal, Stephen realized that for the moment, at least, the Liberal Party was dead. He joined the ranks of the Labour Party. . . . But the Labour Party did not satisfy Stephen. He found it less open to new ideas, more hidebound by tradition than its great and powerful rival. The Conservatives, on the other hand, were on the lookout for a promising young talent" (*Remembered Death,* 44). Political parties are not selected for their platforms and social policies, in this instance, but simply for their instrumentality. As these examples collectively demonstrate, hints of Christie's conservatism appear in her fiction mostly through tortuous routes.

Whereas Christie mutes her conservative leanings in her fictions, she consistently satirizes the English as starchy, stuffy, and insular—in effect, employing the stereotype of the conservative English to mock the nation and its citizenry for their very Englishness. In one such instance she depicts her English characters as interpersonally frosty—"True to their nationality, the two English people were not chatty" (*Orient Express,* 7)—and a French doctor diagnoses the country's citizens as sexually repressed: "The English have a complex about sex.

They think it is 'not quite nice'" (*Appointment with Death*, 54). Poirot frequently derides the English for their insularity, and it is etymologically insightful to consider the English roots of this term that derives from the Latin *insularis,* via the French *insulaire.* The *Oxford English Dictionary* defines the term as "Pertaining to islanders; *esp.* having the characteristic traits of the inhabitants of an island (e.g. of Great Britain); cut off from intercourse with other nations, isolated; self-contained; narrow or prejudiced in feelings, ideas, or manners."[5] The English, within Christie's ironic portrayals, represent an unquestioned cultural norm yet cannot accurately see themselves owing to their insular limitations. As Poirot observes, "I am sure they think that English doctors are the only doctors in the world. Insularity accounts for a lot" (*Poirot Loses a Client,* 129), as he also mocks the English as inveterately immature: "The Anglo Saxon, he takes nothing seriously but playing games! He does not grow up" (*Death on the Nile,* 70). Mr. Satterthwaite, one of Christie's recurring characters, denounces the insularity of his fellow citizens: "Poor old Melrose was so very British in his outlook. Agreeably conscious himself of a cosmopolitan point of view, Mr. Satterthwaite was able to deplore the insular attitude toward life" ("The Love Detective," *Three Blind Mice,* 195–96).

Particularly egregious enactments of insularity expose English racism and xenophobia, which several characters denounce. Poirot refers to Hastings's "insular prejudice against the Argentines, the Portuguese and the Greeks" (*Poirot Loses a Client,* 138); readers are left to discern the uncomfortable irony that Hastings takes his prejudices to Argentina when he relocates there. "Foreigners are so much more precocious than English girls," states one character, to which her indomitable interlocutor sharply replies, "Don't be so insular. . . . We've had plenty of English girls trying to make unsuitable assignations" (*Cat among the Pigeons,* 78). English insularity is further evident in Christie's depictions of juries eager to scapegoat foreigners, including when Poirot is implicated as the killer but the coroner refuses this flagrant, prejudiced injustice: "What's all this? . . . Nonsense. I can't accept this verdict" (*Death in the Air,* 40). Detective Inspector Bland is disappointed but unsurprised by the unexamined prejudices of the local populace: "Bland reflected that the local verdict seemed to be the comfortable and probably agelong one of attributing every tragic occurrence to unspecified foreigners" (*Dead Man's Folly,* 72). In one of his most pointed barbs, Poirot murmurs to himself, "In verity, there are some Englishmen who are altogether so unpleasing and ridiculous that they should have been put out of their misery at birth" (*Patriotic Murders,* 7).

Further relevant to these points, it should be stressed that, in her characterizations of England and English cultural norms, Christie does not view Great Britain as populated by an integrated citizenry, not truly as a United Kingdom; instead, she mostly overlooks any broad concept of the British—one that would, by definition, be inclusive of the Welsh, Scottish, and northern Irish—to focus almost exclusively on the English, as evident in the casual libels directed at the nation's non-English citizenry. Unless otherwise informed, readers know simply to assume that her characters are English born-and-bred, and any characters identified as Welsh, Scottish, or Irish are frequently depicted in disparaging, if ostensibly comic, terms. Ariadne Oliver cries, "I never trust the Welsh! I had a Welsh nurse and she took me to Harrogate one day and went home, having forgotten all about me" (*Cards on the Table*, 78), and *Spider's Web* depicts its protagonists smirking at the Welsh accent of a constable (57). When a lawyer is examining a witness, he undercuts her honesty by employing tired Irish stereotypes: "You're Irish, I think? . . . And the Irish have rather a vivid imagination, haven't they?" (*Sad Cypress*, 173). Tuppence thinks: "Oh, damn, damn, damn the Irish! . . . Why have they got that terrible power of twisting things until you don't know where you are?" (*N or M?* 122). A character in *The Patriotic Murders* derides Scotland as populated wholly with irritable citizens—"The Scotch are always touchy" (141)—although another character concedes, "The Scotch are very independent and one respects them for it" (130). Their characterization as a "patient, dogged people, the Scots" explains why one is suspected of murder in *The Unexpected Guest* (41), and *Sleeping Murder* features a brief but stereotype-laden assessment of a character: "He's a hardheaded, shrewd unemotional Scotsman" (58). The Welsh, Irish, and Scottish may be recognized as citizens of Great Britain, and thus as British, but within Christie's fictions, they do not trouble any presumption that English people and English traditions define the United Kingdom's cultural norms.

For the most part Christie portrays her wealthy, white English characters as insularly ensconced in a nation that respects their cultural authority, and when change is noted, it is almost invariably lamented. Many affluent characters express their discontent with the shifting social landscape, preferring the past when more rigid economic castes reigned; they look longingly back to "the days before money swept aside all class distinctions" (*Crooked House*, 15) and fondly recall the deference formerly afforded them, bewailing that "no loyalty [is found] any more in the lower classes" (*Funerals Are Fatal*, 62). On several occasions Miss Marple laments modernity's encroachments on the old-world charms of St. Mary Mead, such as when she muses inwardly over "the new housing developments. The additions to the Village Hall, the altered appearance of the High Street with its up-to-date shop fronts" and then states reluctantly, "One has to accept change, I suppose" (*At Bertram's Hotel*, 9). In a similar moment, she notes the village's location as "about twenty-five miles from London" and adds: "It used to be a very pretty old-world village, but of course like everything else, it is becoming what they call developed nowadays" (*Nemesis*, 77). Characters similarly condemn evidence of shifting cultural mores, such as when

Christie alludes to such trailblazing mid-century fashion designers as Jacques Fath and Christian Dior (*Dead Man's Folly*, 98), but Miss Marple's friend Ruth Van Rydock, slightly shocked, inquires: "My dear, have you seen what Christian Dior is trying to make us wear in the way of skirts?" (*Murder with Mirrors*, 6). Modern musicians are similarly dismissed when an investigator evinces little knowledge or interest in twentieth-century composers: "Hindemith? Who's he? Never heard of him. Shostakovich? What names these people have"; he then expresses his preference for Handel (*Murder with Mirrors*, 133).

As Christie confessed that she could not write about miners talking in pubs because she did not know what miners talk about in pubs, she likewise admitted, through her alter ego of Ariadne Oliver, that she knew little of "beatniks and sputniks and squares and the beat generation" and then justified her decision largely to overlook them in her fiction: "I don't write about them because I'm so afraid of getting the terms wrong. It's safer, I think, to stick to what you know" (*Pale Horse*, 11–12). Indeed, Oliver's list is an amusing assortment in itself, as she lumps together beatniks first with space technology and then with "squares," who, by definition, they were not. As the decades passed, Christie increasingly alluded to scientific innovations and the onset of the space age but often simply to depict children's amusements. Boys read "the latest space fiction" (*What Mrs. McGillicuddy Saw!* 47), and young Ernie Curtin replicates "a rocket ship going through outer space on its way to Venus" in his play time (*Clocks*, 35). A mother reports that her son said, "Mum I've seen a sputnik, it's come down" (*Ordeal by Innocence*, 168), but it was actually a bubble car. Within Christie's conventional and insular England, change is grudgingly or passingly acknowledged, rarely welcomed, and most evident in children's play. As a further example of Christie's suspicions of change and innovation, supermarkets are not appreciated for their convenience and vast array of products, as lamented by Aunt Matilda in *Passenger to Frankfurt*: "Our own grocer . . . turned suddenly into a supermarket, six times the size, all rebuilt, baskets and wire trays to carry round and try to fill up with things you don't want and mothers always losing their babies, and crying and having hysterics" (24).

Even if England's insular voices would prefer to preserve the status quo, the twentieth century registered a wide array of changes for the nation and its people, particularly concerning their geopolitical preeminence. England's imperialist ambitions, even if never altogether abandoned, withered over the years of Christie's career as many former colonies asserted their independence, including South Africa in 1931, India and Pakistan in 1947, Nigeria in 1960, Zambia in 1964, and Singapore in 1965, among many others. In a likely alignment with her political conservatism, Christie mostly endorses England's imperialist past and present, acknowledging this legacy through affirmations and passing descriptions of characters who lived abroad and then returned home. One character proudly proclaims the honorable ambitions behind English imperialism: "it is, after all, a great thing to be an Englishman. Honesty. That's what we stand for. The Navy has carried that ideal all over the world" (*Why Didn't They Ask Evans?* 30). Many characters who lived in (former) British colonies but then returned to England are referred to as *pukka sahibs,* which the *Oxford English Dictionary* defines as "a person (usually a man) of good family, ability, or credentials; one who is socially acceptable" and notes its etymological roots in Panjabi and Hindi.[6] As a cultural import from the British Raj, the term suggests a comfort with the imperialist mission, evident when Lady Frances Derwent comments on a murder victim: "The dead man was—well, it sounds a most awful thing to say and just like some deadly old retired Anglo-Indian—but the dead man was a pukka sahib" (*Why Didn't They Ask Evans?* 47). In *Passenger to Frankfurt* the indomitable Aunt Matilda assesses the end of British imperialism and compliments the nation for suspending such global aspirations: "We were good at running an empire. We weren't good at *keeping* an empire running, but then you see we didn't need an empire anymore. And we recognized that. Too difficult to keep up" (59). Sounding this nostalgic note, Aunt Matilda now sees England's colonial legacy as an unnecessary encumbrance on the nation but not one that in any way need be regretted.

In a striking irony, the English, as a legacy of their imperialism, might be expected to embrace the diverse citizenry of a multicultural world, but in a telling passage Amy Leatheran, the sympathetic narrator of *Murder in Mesopotamia,* says of Poirot: "I knew he was a foreigner, but I hadn't expected him to be *quite* as foreign as he was, if you know what I mean" (72). Such an assessment of Poirot in England would reflect the nation's insularity, but this novel occurs, as the title indicates, in the Middle East, not in England, and so Amy Leatheran displays the casual arrogance of the English person who cannot see herself ever inhabiting the role of the "foreigner," even when traveling in a distant land. In a similarly ironic moment Poirot comments on the citizens of diverse nationalities residing in the United States: "only in America. In America there might be a household composed of just such varied nationalities—an Italian chauffeur, an English governess, a Swedish nurse, a German lady's maid, and so on" (*Orient Express,* 203)—despite what one might presume would be the greater propensity of these nationalities to congregate in England, given its proximity.

In a manner similar to her treatment of imperialistic themes, Christie's presentation of a predominantly white England showcases a casually pernicious racism. Two characters enjoying their date share their mutual antipathies— "They disliked loud voices, noisy restaurants and Negroes" (*Death in the Air,* 115)—and one of the suspects in *Cards on the Table* declares, "I never forget a face—even a black face, and that's a lot more than most people can say" (99). Mr. Parker Pyne masterminds a scenario in which his client encounters a distressing scene—"There in the shrubbery was a girl struggling in the grasp of two enormous Negroes" (*Parker Pyne*, 21)—but even if this scene is staged, it nonetheless relies on troubling racist visions of Black men preying on white women. Again, as with so many other elements of Christie's fiction, it is important to consider the ways in which her characterizations influence readers' interpretations of their potential motives for murder. For example, in *And Then There Were None*, the adventurer Lombard denies the fundamental humanity of nonwhite peoples—"And natives don't mind dying, you know. They don't feel about it as Europeans do" (44)—whereas Emily Brent speaks in the words of a humanitarian: "Black or white, they are our brothers" (70). Both Lombard and Brent are murdered for their past actions, rendering the latter's recognition of racial fellowship a sign of her rigid thinking rather than of her enlightenment.

In a telling sign of her comfort with racist epithets, Christie frequently used the n-word, most notably in the original title of *And Then There Were None* as *Ten Little N------*. Despite its later retitling, as Blake Allmendinger notes, "Christie referred to the novel by its original title in her autobiography, published posthumously in 1977 . . . [and editions] of the novel featuring the original title continued to be published in the United Kingdom until 1980."[7] Christie frequently employed the phrase "a n----- in the woodpile" (*Poirot Loses a Client*, 139; cf. *And Then There Were None*, 25, 76; *Murder with Mirrors*, 101; *Funerals Are Fatal*, 192), but toward the end of her career, she replaced it with "Indian in the woodpile" (*Passenger to Frankfurt*, 202) in a benighted attempt to employ less offensive language.

Toward the end of the twentieth century, one of England's ostensibly defining norms—whiteness—could no longer assert the overwhelming force of its cultural hegemony. Of Christie's novels, *Hickory Dickory Death*, set in a boarding house for university students, most cleary envisions a newly multicultural England, but only partially, for many of these students are foreseen as returning to their homelands. The novel commences as Miss Lemon observes England's changing racial demographics—"'Half the nurses in our hospitals seem to be black nowadays,' said Miss Lemon, doubtfully"—with the adverb "doubtfully" indicating her discomfort, perhaps even distaste, yet she then adds, "and I understand much pleasanter and more attentive than the English ones" (4). Miss Lemon's distinction between the nurses as Black or as English tacitly indicates her presumption that whiteness defines Englishness.

This novel contains several seesawing passages in which one character expresses a racist viewpoint that another then rebuts. When Mrs. Nicoletis, the hostel's owner, proposes that all of the nonwhite tenants should be evicted—"And if it is these coloured students, these Indians, these Negresses—then they can all go, you understand?"—Mrs. Hubbard, the hostel's manager, indignantly replies: "Not while I'm in charge" (20). One character identifies another as a racist while exculpating the other boarders from this charge—"I think he might have a bit of racial feeling. About the only one of us who has" (82)—but then a different character disproves this point: "All these coloured people are very jealous of each other and very hysterical" (91). Elizabeth Johnson, from Jamaica, is referred to as "Black Bess," with the narrator adding, "The nickname was an affectionate one and had been accepted as such by the girl herself" (22), and the nonwhite characters discuss the implications and limitations of the phrase "free, white, and twenty-one" (56). *Hickory Dickory Death* also features Mr. Akibombo from West Africa, who is played for humor when in an interview with Inspector Sharpe he "gave a most realistic and gigantic belch" to demonstrate his digestive ailments (175). In a concluding image of racial harmony, Mr. Akibombo is invited to be the best man at the future wedding of two white characters (197), yet it is one in which, by definition, he must stand to the side of them. Christie adumbrates interracial and interethnic marriages in some of her later novels, including the pairing of Tina Argyle and Michael Argyle at the conclusion of *Ordeal by Innocence* and of Alice Calder and Ali Yusuf in *Cat among the Pigeons*.

While the blanket assumption of English whiteness holds true for the vast majority of Christie's novels, any presumption of a norm of moral whiteness is travestied by the fact that these books uniformly feature white murderers. In a strikingly mordant instance of these dynamics, Colonel Race opines why a particular suspect would not likely be the killer: "I'd lay long odds against its being Despard. He's a white man, Battle." Superintendent Battle replies, "Incapable of murder, you mean?" to which Colonel Race agrees, "Incapable of what I'd call murder—yes" (*Cards on the Table*, 122). Colonel Race's name ironically underscores his interest in racial profiling and his obdurate defense of whiteness as a virtue, yet surely virtually every reader, no matter how baffled they might be by Christie's puzzle, would nonetheless correctly presume that the killer would be white, given the overwhelming whiteness of her casts of characters. Colonel Race is proved correct in his defense of John Despard but incorrect in his defense of white men, one of whom is the murderer in *Cards on the Table*. A similar instance of ethnic profiling occurs in *A Holiday for Murder*. Pilar Estravados, a character who is half-Spanish and half-English, trots out tired stereotypes of both nationalities: "In Spain they take out their knives and they curse and shout. In England they do nothing, just get very red in the face and shut up their mouths tight" (105). Building on such stereotypes, another character implicates Pilar by suggesting that the murder—a throat-slashing—was "so very *un*-English"; Poirot understands the insinuation: "Ah . . . the Spanish touch, you think" (126). Despite this character's attempt to pin the crime on Pilar by appealing to English bigotries, it turns out that the murder, and the murderer as well, were not "so very *un*-English" after all.

Against these backdrops of imperialism and the assumed cultural normativity of English whiteness, Christie condemns English insularity through a particularly ingenious narrative strategy for creating such appealing fiction: her most famous detectives, Hercule Poirot and Miss Marple, act as queer foils who highlight the inability of normative English culture to perceive its hidebound traditions and prejudices. Because Hercule Poirot and Miss Marple stand outside the insular ranks of the English, owing to the advanced age and nationality of the former and the advanced age and gender of the latter, they are more memorable and appealing protagonists than those of many of her predecessors, her contemporaries, and her successors in the field of detective fiction, as evidenced by such authors and detectives as R. Austin Freeman's Dr. Thorndyke, Ngaio Marsh's Roderick Alleyn, and P. D. James's Adam Dalgleish. For instance, Freeman said of Dr. Thorndyke: "As he was a man of acute intellect and sound judgment, I kept Thorndyke free of eccentricities, perfectly sane and normal."[8] Without any distinguishing personality quirks, Thorndyke simply represents a white male English character among a sea of other such characters. Ngaio Marsh introduced Alleyn through the eyes of another character: "Alleyn did not resemble a plain-clothes policeman she felt sure, nor was he in the romantic manner—white faced and gimlet-eyed. He looked like one of her Uncle Hubert's friends, the sort that they knew would 'do' for house-parties."[9] In other words, Alleyn belongs comfortably, if somewhat jauntily, to the social class and society that he is called upon to investigate. P. D. James's Dalgleish similarly fits into the investigative department to which he is assigned: "Dalgliesh, as a permanent ADC [Assistant District Commissioner] to the Commissioner, had a number of functions which, as they grew in number and importance, had become so ill-defined that most of his colleagues had given up trying to define them."[10] Thorndyke, Alleyn, and Dalgleish sport some individualizing touches—Thorndyke's background in medicine, Alleyn's spry humor, Dalgleish's forays in poetry—yet, as white, straight, financially comfortable men, they enjoy the prerogatives of their privilege and the deference afforded them by others.

Christie succumbed to similarly nondescript characters several times, but her white, straight, financially comfortable detectives (e.g., Parker Pyne, Superintendent Battle) are simply less memorable than Hercule Poirot and Miss Marple. Indeed, the name of "Detective Inspector Bland" in *Dead Man's Folly* indicates that he is unremarkable and destined to be outshined by Poirot, and thus that he need display little more than the blandest of personalities. Even when Christie features Superintendent Battle as the primary detective in *Towards Zero,* he alludes to Poirot's obsession with symmetry, which then helps him to determine the correct murder weapon. In sum, even many of the finest mystery writers of the twentieth century did little to individualize their detectives as distinct from their wider culture, in contrast to the noteworthy features of Hercule Poirot and Miss Marple that sharpen Christie's critiques of English insularity.

Further relevant to the queer touches of Christie's novels, Michael Moon points out that "Christie's two main series detectives—Hercule Poirot and Jane Marple—are themselves hardly exemplars of twentieth-century models of heterosexuality for their respective genders."[11] On the surface, Poirot appears a confirmed bachelor of heteroerotic orientation. "Me, I always notice when a girl is pretty" (*Dead Man's Mirror*, 108), he chirps, and narrators record his passionate admiration for Countess Vera Rossakoff: "He, Hercule Poirot, remembered women. . . . One woman, in particular—what a sumptuous creature—A Bird of Paradise—a Venus. . . . What woman was there among these pretty chits nowadays, who could hold a candle to Countess Vera Rossakoff?" (*Patriotic Murders*, 162). Another narrator sympathetically hints that Poirot's affections were seldom returned: "It is the misfortune of small, precise men to hanker after large and flamboyant women" ("The Capture of Cerberus," *Labors of Hercules*, 197). Retired from the Belgian police force in his first appearance in *The Mysterious Affair at Styles* and growing older as the novels progress, Poirot appears to have left amatory matters behind, as the narrator reports of his thoughts: "Admittedly there must be love, young people must meet and pair off, but he, Poirot, was mercifully past all that" (*Hickory Dickory Death*, 46). Poirot admits that he is "not of an ardent temperament. It has saved me from many embarrassments" ("The Mystery of the Bagdad Chest," *Regatta*, 26).

Collectively these lines suggest a man of heterosexual orientation aging into celibacy, yet Christie complicates her characterization of Poirot by repeatedly describing him with queer stereotypes. He is mistaken for a "woman's dressmaker" (*Orient Express*, 40), Hastings calls him a "man milliner" (*ABC Murders*, 113), and he looks "like a hairdresser in a comic play" (*Mesopotamia*, 72). Further along these lines, Hastings calls him an "inveterate dandy" ("The Mystery of the Bagdad Chest," *Regatta*, 29), and readers see him "dressed in a dandified fashion in white flannels" ("Triangle at Rhodes," *Dead Man's Mirror*, 205). In late nineteenth-century and twentieth-century Britain and the United States, dandyism upset any presumed borders between heterosexuality and homosexuality. Not all dandies of these eras were queers, and not all queers were dandies, but sufficient interplay of the categories raises the issue of how these many dandies contribute to Christie's characterization of Poirot.[12] Oscar Wilde stands as the definitive exemplar of a queer dandy; Joe Lucchesi observes: "After Oscar Wilde's 1895 sodomy conviction, the image of the elegantly attired gentleman became indelibly associated with decadent male homosexuality."[13] Christie's alter ego Ariadne Oliver avows her protagonist's asexual tendencies— "Sven Hjerson never cared for women"—to which a playwright adapting her novel responds, "But you *can't* have him a *pansy,* darling!" (*McGinty,* 101). One could certainly object that a man who "never cared for women" need not necessarily be a gay man, but the presumptive force of normative heterosexuality is such that, when a man does not adhere to its expectations, he is then interpreted as queer. More so, as much as Christie disliked Hastings and dispatched him to Argentina, Poirot's friendship with him marks them as a homosocially inclined couple. Hastings finds love in *Murder on the Links* but his wife subsequently lingers in the background. "My wife remained to manage the ranch" (*ABC Murders,* 1), he informs readers who might wonder of her absence, and his daughter Judith comments on her father and his longtime friend, "What a funny couple you are" (*Curtain,* 22). Further to these points, Sally Munn observes that Poirot "embodies . . . the 'feminine.' He is a parody of the male myth; his name implies his satirical status; he is a shortened Hercules, and a *poirot*—a clown."[14]

Poirot's idiosyncratic gender and sexuality mark him apart from normative English culture, and he takes advantage of his otherness during his investigations, which thus affords Christie another opportunity to hold England up for critique over its insularity. In a telling passage, the narrator describes "the Hercule Poirot manner," in which the detective has "masked [himself] behind a foreign shield of flattering words and much-increased foreign mannerisms, so that they themselves should feel agreeably contemptuous of him" (*Hallowe'en Party,* 138). Poirot's performed foreignness protects him from other's misperceptions and prejudices; he, in essence, disguises himself as a foreigner (evident in the "much-increased foreign mannerisms"), with the explicit purpose of engendering disdain for himself and thereby disarming these English natives of any defenses they might presumably erect. Compounding this aspect of his character, Poirot deploys his accent to deceive his interlocutors: "It is true that I can speak the exact, the idiomatic English. But, my friend, to speak the broken English is an enormous asset. It leads people to despise you. They say, 'A foreigner; he can't even speak English properly.' It is not my policy to terrify people; instead, I invite their gentle ridicule" (*Three Acts,* 198). The "gentle ridicule" that Poirot solicits traps the English in their very English insularity, with this tactic frequently ensnaring the culprits.

Christie pays even less attention to Miss Marple's erotic biography than she does to Poirot's, but like the Belgian detective, this character's Otherness within English culture allows her to dupe many of her interlocutors and always to identify the killer. Most apparently, her advanced years mark her as estranged from the prevailing norms of society, leading her younger relatives and companions to dismiss her intellect: "they decided that dear Aunt Jane was perhaps getting a *little* bit disconnected in her old age" ("Greenshaw's Folly," *Double Sin,* 123). Like Poirot, Miss Marple is similarly characterized as somewhat queer, even if not necessarily homosexual or bisexual in her orientation. If Christie envisioned a backstory explaining Miss Marple's spinsterhood, she never divulged it, and so this aspect of her background must remain an unknowable void. Thus, to read Miss Marple as a lesbian character would be to overinterpret from the available textual evidence, but, correspondingly, perceiving her as a heterosexual character likewise overinterprets from a pervasive omission of information.

All that can be confidently stated is that Miss Marple enjoys sufficient understanding both of straight and of queer desires to solve the mysteries that she chances upon. As Kathy Mezei observes of literary spinsters, "the spinster is nevertheless uniquely situated as an instrument of surveillance precisely because of her marginal and indeterminate position,"[15] and Miss Marple's knowledge of nonheteronormative sexuality tacitly indicates a range of queer goings-on in St. Mary Mead and beyond. She more often uncovers murderous motivations that are heteroerotic in their orientation, as in her debut novel *The Murder at the Vicarage,* but in explicating the subterranean desires at play in *Nemesis,* she discreetly, but nonetheless clearly, delineates the homoerotic attractions that led to murder. She explains that Clotilde Bradbury-Scott killed Verity Hunt because Verity wanted "to live with the man of her choice, to have children by him. She wanted marriage and the happiness of normality" (*Nemesis* 205). She then expands on these points, detailing that, as Verity matured, she planned to leave behind her relationship with Clotilde: "It was all mapped out so plainly then—the overwhelming love that Clotilde had had for this girl. The girl's hero-worship of her, dependency on her, and then as she grew a little older, her normal instincts came into play" (*Nemesis,* 218).

Miss Marple's focus on "normality" marks lesbianism as the abnormal—and hence we can see Christie's insularity in play—yet Miss Marple's knowledge about lesbianism marks her as more worldly than many readers might originally anticipate. Another Miss Marple mystery, *A Murder Is Announced,* includes passages suggestive of lesbian relationships, primarily in the pairings of Letitia Blacklock and Dora Bunner and of Miss Hincliffe and Miss Murgatroyd. Letitia Blacklock is described by another character in masculine terms: "Letitia, you know, has really got a man's mind. She hasn't any feminine feelings or weaknesses. I don't believe she was ever in love with any man. She used a little make-up in deference to prevailing custom, but not to make herself look prettier. . . . She never knew any of the fun of being a woman" (130). In her letters Letitia describes herself as wholly uninterested in romance, potentially suggesting her asexuality, "I said I didn't think I was likely to fall in love with anybody" (164). Readers see Miss Hinchcliffe and Miss Murgatroyd as devoted companions, and after Miss Murgatroyd's death, Miss Hinchcliffe's mourning registers deeply: "The ravaged face of the tall vigorous woman told its own tale, and would have made any expression of sympathy an impertinence" (194). With *Nemesis* and *A Murder Is Announced* showcasing Christie's deepest excavations of lesbian desire, it is a tangential but compelling piece of evidence that Miss Marple is called upon to resolve their mysteries.

Christie's queer insularity is also evident in her gender politics, as she represents the intriguing case of a woman who achieved an international reputation and fantastic wealth through her work while concomitantly displaying a curious double-mindedness about the question of whether women should, or even should want to, work. The labor of writing appears to have so wholly ingrained itself into Christie's character that she could hardly have stopped had she desired to do so, as evident in the words of the sculptor Henrietta Savernake, who, in *The Hollow,* muses on the creation of her artworks: "Sculpture isn't a thing you set out to do and succeed in. It's a thing that gets *at* you, that nags at you—and haunts you—so that, sooner or later, you've got to make terms with it. And then, for a bit, you get some peace—until the whole thing starts over again" (51). For a woman who began writing after a wager with her sister, who hesitated to call herself an author for almost a decade into her illustrious career, these words illuminate the ways in which words and plots nagged her annually. Notwithstanding her personal work ethic, she wondered why women would seek professional vocations: "The position of women, over the years, has definitely changed for the worse. We women have behaved like mugs. We have clamoured to be allowed to work as men work" (*Autobiography,* 121). More so, in appraising the financial acumen of her father and brother, she noted their failures and her success: "My grandfather made a big fortune. My father, mainly owning to trust in his fellow men, let it dwindle away, and my brother ran through what was left of it like a flash of lightning. I seem to have started up the ladder again, perhaps taking after my grandfather!" (*Autobiography,* 26).

Given this disjunction between Christie's rigorous work ethic and her stated beliefs, it is hardly surprising that her views of gender, as mediated through her fiction, represent a Gordian knot of contradictions and paradoxes, resulting in the virtual impossibility of clearly delineating her views of the feminist advances of the twentieth century. Women's collective intellects and abilities are occasionally denigrated by other women, such as when a female character of approximately sixty years says, "I'm afraid women are never quite such deep thinkers as men" (*Easy to Kill,* 128). Miss Marple sees clear, essentialist distinctions between the sexes: "Accuracy is more a male quality than a female quality" (*Nemesis,* 124). When a woman confidently tells Hercule Poirot, "Woman, M. Poirot, is going to be the great force in Government in ten years' time," his reaction, as recorded by the narrator, suggests his acceptance, or perhaps his resignation, to this prediction: "Poirot said that he was sure of it" ("The Incredible Theft," *Dead Man's Mirror,* 123). In several contrasting instances, Christie sympathetically portrays women's aspirations for fulfilling career opportunities, acknowledging their rather limited options throughout much of the twentieth century, as evidenced by Mary Durrant: "This girl, Mary Durrant, had come to be with her aunt and learn the business and was very excited about it—much preferring it to the other alternative—becoming a nursery governess or companion" ("Double Sin," *Double Sin*, 7). Another woman points out the inherent sexism behind advancing a boy's education over a girl's: "It is incredible to you that women should want a career. It was incredible to my parents. I was anxious to study for a doctor. They would not hear of paying the fees. But they paid them readily for Owen. Yet I should have made a better doctor than my brother" (*Moving Finger*, 45). In a particularly chilling moment, Honoria Waynflete confesses that sexism played a significant role in the frustrations that led her to murder: "Yes, I always had brains, even as a girl. But they wouldn't let me do anything. I had to stay at home, doing nothing" (*Easy to Kill*, 182). During the boredom she was compelled to endure grew the seeds of her homicidal inclinations.

Further complicating Christie's gender politics, her novels quietly endorse women's rights to reproductive autonomy through abortion but question the reality of rape. "Girls in trouble" appear with relative frequency in Christie's canon, perhaps most famously with the case of Emily Brent's maid in *And Then There Were None*. This young woman died by suicide after Brent dismissed her for her pregnancy, but Brent's callous cruelty justifies the killer's selection of her as one of his victims.[16] As Miss Marple knows about lesbianism, she also knows about premarital sex and its potential repercussions. "And sure enough poor Florrie was in trouble" (*A Murder Is Announced*, 122), she states, and in another of her cases, she says to her maid Edna about Edna's cousin Gladdie: "Dear me . . . Not—not in trouble?" ("The Case of the Perfect Maid," *Three Blind Mice*, 105). By and large, these unmarried pregnant women are treated with sympathy and concern, including when Miss Bulstrode does not fire a teacher employed at her school for her "trouble" and summarizes the challenging situation that this young woman faced: "There was a man, you fell in love with him, you had a child. I suppose you couldn't marry" (*Cat among the Pigeons*, 213–14). Sometimes "girls in trouble" would benefit from an abortion, a possibility that Christie treats sensitively when a character recalls the unjust fate of a local doctor: "We still call him Dr. Stokes although he's been struck off. A very nice man he is, embittered a bit, of course, by being struck off. It was only his kind heart really, helping a lot of girls who were no better than they should be" (*At Bertram's Hotel*, 115).

In another example of these dynamics, Christie's short story "The Water Bus" features the hypocritically religious character Mrs. Hargreaves who feels little sympathy for the plight of her maid's daughter, as reported by the mother: "Just goes off to this awful place—and how she heard about it, I don't know—and this wicked woman did things to her, and it went septic—or whatever they call it— and they took her off to Hospital and she's lying there now, *dying . . .* Won't say who the man was—not even now" ("The Water Bus," *Star over Bethlehem*, 24).

In a similar passage Christie writes that Mrs. Jarrow "had tried two doctors with the idea of having an abortion, but did not succeed in finding one who would perform what was then an illegal operation" (*Elephants Can Remember,* 147). Notably, these latter references to abortion occur toward the end of Christie's career—*At Bertram's Hotel* was published in 1965, *Star over Bethlehem* in 1965, and *Elephants Can Remember* in 1972—reflecting her assessment of contemporary debates on the topic. The Abortion Act of 1967 legalized abortion in England, Wales, and Scotland.

In contrast to these sympathetic views on pregnant, unmarried women and the liberal views expressed on abortion, Christie mostly overlooks rape as a potential story line or plot device. Murders occur in nearly all of her fiction, but sexual violence rarely darkens her pages. In contrast to this prevailing absence, Christie speaks repeatedly but dismissively of rape in *Nemesis.* One character states: "Girls, you must remember, are far more ready to be raped nowadays than they used to be. Their mothers insist, very often, that they should call it rape" (*Nemesis,* 110). Some pages later, another character offers an extended version of such views: "Well, we all know what rape is nowadays. Mum tells the girl she's got to accuse the young man of rape even if the young man hasn't had much chance, with the girl at him all the time to come to the house while Mum's away at work or Dad's gone on holiday. Doesn't stop badgering him until she's forced him to sleep with her. Then, as I say, Mum tells the girl to call it rape" (133). Both of these characters are men, yet their perspectives are not meaningfully questioned or challenged.

Christie pays only passing attention to homosexuality and queer identities in her novels, yet their deeper thematic relevance arises in the unknowability of suspects' motivations for their actions, in the undercurrents of unexpressed yet vibrant desires. Foremost, it is at times difficult to discern precisely what Christie means by the word *queer,* as illustrated in the following passage from *Murder with Mirrors.* This novel is set in an institution for delinquent boys, and the character Gina Hudd expresses her distaste for them: "I don't fancy the queers so much. Of course, Lewis and Dr Maverick think they're *all* queers— I mean they think it's repressed desires and disordered home life and their mothers getting off with soldiers and all that" (18). It seems unlikely that Gina believes that all of the inmates are gay and is instead suggesting that they all suffer from some sort of mental disorder, a possibility that gains further credence when she later suggests: "But one of the queers—you know, what they call mentally maladjusted—might do it for fun, don't you think?" (120). *Queer* does not necessarily denote, or even connote, *gay* in Christie's fictions, but because homosexuality was classified as a mental illness for much of the twentieth century, Gina Hudd's mishmashed assessments of the delinquent boys showcases the overlap between the two.

At other times in Christie's fiction, it is possible to read queer subtexts that were perhaps unintended or were simply left undeveloped. For example, in *Passenger to Frankfurt* Sir Stafford Nye reads the personal ads in a newspaper and comes across the following: "Young man who objects to hard work and who would like an easy life would be glad to undertake a job that would suit him" (38). Such an advertisement would seem to be offering the services of a sex worker—a rent boy, in the popular parlance—but this possibility is not explored as the novel unwinds. As with many of Christie's allusions to queer characters and queer desires, it is mentioned in passing as the story then marches on.

Any comparison between queer people of the twentieth century and Christie's murderers is not a flattering one, yet it reflects the coded nature of much queer life during this period: quite simply, many queers and virtually all murderers had a secret they desperately wanted to keep. In searching for traces of queer characters in Christie's fictions beyond the examples of *A Murder Is Announced* and *Nemesis,* several men, similar to Hercule Poirot, could be described as queerly straight. Christie does not label them as gay or depict them engaging in demonstrably homoerotic behaviors, but she unpacks any presumption that heteronormativity might capture the vast array of male gender performances. For example, Mr. Christopher Wren in *Three Blind Mice* appears to be a gay connoisseur, which is hinted at when he scrutinizes furniture for its aesthetic appeal, when a male character expresses blatant, likely homophobic, hostility toward him, and when a female character calls him "a very peculiar young man" (14). Wren comments on Detective Trotter's physical appeal: "He's very handsome, don't you think so? I always think policemen are terribly attractive" (33). Mr. Satterthwaite, who appears in *The Mysterious Mr. Quin, Murder in Three Acts,* and some short stories, embodies several gendered paradoxes: "For a manly man, Mr. Satterthwaite knew far too much about women. There was a womanish strain in his character which lent him insight into the feminine mind. Woman all his life had confided in him, but they had never taken him seriously" (*Three Acts,* 11). A woman tells Mr. Sattherthwaite that he is "half a woman" (*Mr. Quin,* 200). A "manly man" with "a womanish strain" whom women never perceive as a likely romantic partner, Mr. Satterthwaite seems queer without being defined as such. In another intriguing moment, Egg says candidly, "I like men to have affairs . . . It shows they're not queer or anything," following which the narrator records his reaction: "Mr. Satterthwaite's Victorianism suffered a further pang" (*Three Acts,* 26). Does the arrow hit too close to any closeted desires that Mr. Satterthwaite might have buried?

Christie's characters inhabit an unquestionably cisgendered world, aside from a few characters who cross-dress, often for notorious purposes. *The Man in the Brown Suit* features Miss Pettigrew, of whom another character snipes: "There is nothing attractive about Miss Pettigrew—she is a repellent female with large feet, more like a man than a woman" (*Brown Suit*, 183; cf. 269). In actuality, "Miss Pettigrew" is the assumed identity of Arthur Minks, a man who impersonates a range of identities, including the Reverend Edward Chichester and Count Sergius Paulovitch. In *Partners in Crime* the criminal mastermind No. 16 disguises himself as Mrs. Van Snyder (213). Christie also depicts women cross-dressing as men, such as entertainer and male impersonator Kitty Kidd, who plays a small role in the duplicities of *The Mystery of the Blue Train* (202). In explicating the solution to a mystery, Poirot explains that "The tall, deep-voiced Mrs. Rice is a very successful male impersonator" ("The Stymphalean Birds," *Labors of Hercules*, 111). Christie mostly employs cross-dressing not to explore the interiority of a character's gendered identity but simply as a ruse in a criminal act, but at the same time, readers might wonder how these characters discovered their talents for such convincing cross-dressing. David Hunter, a suspect in *There Is a Tide* . . . who impersonates a woman to avoid suspicion, says of himself: "I think a good deal of myself as a female impersonator" (207). Surely readers must therefore imagine David Hunter practicing this talent and seeking to enhance the illusion that his performances create, and thus wonder as well of his personal motivations for pursuing this goal.

Christie's queer insularity reflects the personal circumstances of her life and times, the historical trajectory of the twentieth century, and her compelling critique of Englishness, even if Englishness is mostly valorized as her characters' default normative identity. For many readers, Christie's queer insularity may not overwrite the troubling aspects of her fiction, while other readers will contextualize these elements as part of her milieu and its insufficiently examined prejudices. For instance, the word "retarded" has fallen out of favor for describing people with intellectual disabilities, but Christie's use of it simply reflects its unquestioned acceptance during much of her lifetime, when "mental retardation" was used as a medical term. Her play *The Unexpected Guest* includes a character with an intellectual disability, and it now begins with the publisher's disclaimer, titled "Notes on Sensitive Terminology," which states that "Language used by the author in her stage directions and by her characters to describe mental and physical conditions and disabilities is of the period in which the play was first performed" and which encourages "directors and actors to interpret" these passages in respect to their personal vision (vi). The disclaimer included with *Spider's Web* expands on such points: "Language used by the author in her stage directions and by her characters to describe religion, gender, sexuality, race and class is of the period in which the play was first performed" (vi). Clearly individual readers must determine for themselves whether the historical conditions of a novel's production offer sufficient contextualization for any insensitive treatment of benighted prejudices, as they must simultaneously assess the ways in which Christie reflected and resisted the cultural mores of her lifetime.

As this chapter demonstrates, Christie privileges assumed English norms (of wealth, whiteness, and heterosexuality) while creating sufficient space to critique them as reflective of English insularity and ignorance. In an apt concluding example of these dynamics, one character says disparagingly to Miss Marple of an American, "He's young, crude, and he comes from a country where a man is esteemed by the success he makes of life," to which Miss Marple replies with tart innocence: "Whilst here we are so very fond of failures" (*Murder with Mirrors,* 96). Precisely because of its assumptions of wealth, whiteness, and heterosexuality, England abounds in such failures, even as Christie's queer insularity ironically highlights them for readers both inside and outside of English norms.

EIGHT

Christie's Murders at the Movies . . . and Why She Disliked Them

Agatha Christie's legacy rests on her individual efforts in penning her many dozens of novels and short stories, yet it is undoubtedly bolstered by the ambitions of a wide array of creative talents, dating from the late 1920s to today, who have adapted her mysteries for the cinema, theatre, and other entertainment media. Here again arises a great paradox in Christie's continuing reception because she squirmed at the purported indignities to which her novels were subjected when transformed into theatrical and cinematic productions—a point recorded in public statements and thematized in her fiction. "I had no idea when the idea was first suggested what terrible suffering you go through with plays, owing to the alterations made in them," she stated in her *Autobiography* (421). Sounding a similar note, her alter ego Ariadne Oliver ruefully comments on a stage adaptation of one of her novels: "you've no idea of the agony of having your characters taken and made to say things that they never would have said, and do things that they never would have done. And if you protest, all they say is that it's 'good theatre'" (*McGinty*, 77). In a condensed expression of these viewpoints, an incidental character remarks upon "the eternal surprise of the author at what the producer has done to him" (*Pale Horse*, 37). Christie's interest in scriptwriting can be largely credited to her disappointment with early theatrical stagings of her stories and her ambition to reformat her fiction to her satisfaction, evident in her adaptations of *And Then There Were None*, *Hidden Horizon* (her adaptation of *Death on the Nile*), *Appointment with Death*, *Towards Zero*, *The Hollow*, *Witness for the Prosecution*, and *Go Back for Murder* (her adaptation of *Murder in Retrospect*).

As Christie's dismay over adaptations of her works suggests, film and television adaptations are both inspired and haunted by their sources, and the field of adaptation studies grapples with this dualistic tension. Deborah Cartmell and

Imelda Whelehan lament the field's "tendency to foreground the literary in a nod to its still privileged cultural status" as they also "wonder whether focusing on the 'films themselves' is possible or desirable when studying the process of adaptation."[1] In their new role as viewers of a theatrical or cinematic production, readers of the original text invariably compare and contrast the original to the adaptation, pondering what was changed, for what reasons, and what effects were achieved by these changes. The resulting conundrum of whether such alterations enhance or vandalize the source text stands as the defining issue in interpreting adaptations. The crux of adaptations, then, is that many viewers expect them to adhere faithfully to the contours of the source text despite the inherent challenges of doing so. In the transition from page to stage or screen, stories inevitably shift but to staggeringly different degrees.

More so, murder mysteries present unique challenges to screenwriters, as Otto Penzler notes: "To be fair, it's very difficult to put a good detective story on screen and make a good detective movie. . . . Most of what happens is cerebral—observing clues, making deductions—and that's hard to portray in an exciting manner on screen. It's just a different medium."[2] Often characters and plot points are cut in the transition from Christie's novels of roughly 200 pages to movies of roughly two hours, and frequently the complexity of the crimes must be simplified as well. For many readers, the chief attraction of murder mysteries arises in the puzzles that authors have created, with interpretive pleasure sparked as they match wits with fictional detectives. Adaptations dramatizing these narratives, whether on stage or screen, face the difficulty of imbuing deeper emotional resonance to a cerebral challenge populated, for the most part, with characters requiring simply a reasonable motive for murder rather than a fully drawn emotional core. Beatrix Hesse hypothesizes that "the detective novel is mainly interested in Knowledge, [whereas] the crime play is more concerned with Emotion," with her words suggesting the challenges of successfully adapting such a source text to a new medium.[3] Furthermore, many mystery novels, notwithstanding the emotional impact of a murder or other such heinous crime, often metamorphose into a somewhat static narrative trajectory, in which the detective simply interviews the various suspects. A story that begins with a shocking action devolves into a series of conversations, and such a rigid narrative structure would, in many ways, appear unamenable to the visual and kinetic nature of film.

As her international reputation grew in the 1920s, Christie's fiction was increasingly adapted to the cinematic and theatrical realms.[4] Early film adaptions of her fiction include *The Passing of Mr. Quin* in 1928 and the German film *Die Abenteur GmbH,* an adaptation of *The Secret Adversary* released in 1929. *The Murder of Roger Ackroyd* was staged as *Alibi* in 1928, with Charles Laughton as Poirot, and then released as a film, also titled *Alibi,* in 1931, with Austin Trevor as Poirot. Trevor also portrayed Poirot in *Black Coffee* (1931) and *Lord Edgeware Dies* (1934), thereby becoming the first of many actors to cement their star status through their connection to Christie vehicles. In the 1930s Christie collaborated with the BBC on radio productions and even early television productions, including *The Wasp's Nest* (1937) and *Love from a Stranger* (1938, an adaptation of her short story "Philomel Cottage"). Prominent adapted films over the next decades include René Clair's *And Then There Were None* (1945), Richard Whorf's *Love from a Stranger* (1947), Billy Wilder's *Witness for the Prosecution* (1957), and Godfrey Grayson's *The Spider's Web* (1960). Adaptations of Christie's novels accelerated in the 1960s when she signed a contract with MGM, which inaugurated a string of films starring Margaret Rutherford as Miss Marple. Christie subsequently dedicated *The Mirror Crack'd* to Rutherford but also stated: "Margaret Rutherford . . . is a very good actress, but she is nothing like the character that I made."[5] Rutherford's career as Miss Marple comprises four films: *Murder, She Said* (1961, inspired by *What Mrs. McGillicuddy Saw!*); *Murder at the Gallop* (1963, inspired by *Funerals Are Fatal*); *Murder Most Foul* (1964, inspired by *Mrs. McGinty's Dead*); and *Murder Ahoy* (1964, which was not based on a Christie story). MGM also released *The Alphabet Murders* (1965), a farcical take on one of Christie's most chilling tales that features a particularly odd casting decision: Tony Randall as Poirot, with this famed character now proving himself a surprisingly seasoned bowler and adept yoga practitioner. The film also recasts the first two victims as a water clown and a bowling instructor, instead of a tobacconist and a waitress, in a clear indication that its creators aimed to translate one of Christie's tautest and most chilling novels into broad comedy. Christie regretted her partnership with MGM: "I really feel sick and ashamed of what I did when I joined up with MGM. It was my fault. One does things for money and one is wrong to do so—since one parts with one's literary integrity."[6]

The 1970s witnessed the rise of Christie adaptations as extravagant productions populated by all-star casts, beginning with Sidney Lumet's *Murder on the Orient Express* (1974), which features Albert Finney as Hercule Poirot, with Ingrid Bergman, Lauren Bacall, Sean Connery, and Anthony Perkins in supporting roles. Following this blockbuster success, John Guillermin directed *Death on the Nile* (1978), in which Peter Ustinov undertook the role of Hercule Poirot for the first time of many, with Mia Farrow, Bette Davis, Maggie Smith, David Niven, and Angela Lansbury among the supporting cast. This trend continued in the 1980s with Guy Hamilton's *The Mirror Crack'd* (1980), with Angela Lansbury as Miss Marple, and his *Evil under the Sun* (1982), with Ustinov returning as Poirot. Christie novels were frequently aired on American television in the 1980s; for example, Helen Hayes played Miss Marple in two television movies —*A Caribbean Mystery* (1983) and *Murder with Mirrors* (1985)—as well as appearing in *Murder Is Easy* (1982). Across the Atlantic Ocean the BBC produced

Miss Marple from 1984 to 1992, adapting twelve of the Miss Marple novels. For many Christie fans, Joan Hickson's performance in the title role stands as the definitive screen interpretation of Miss Marple. (Oddly, or presciently, enough, Christie foresaw this sterling alignment of actor and role, as she congratulated Hickson with a note following her performance as Miss Pryce in the 1945 staging of *Appointment with Death:* "I hope one day you will play my dear Miss Marple."[7]) Such a surfeit of adaptations in the 1970s and 1980s partially explains the disappointing results of Michael Winner's *Appointment with Death* (1988), another film in the blockbuster tradition, with Ustinov as Poirot and featuring Lauren Bacall, Carrie Fisher, Piper Laurie, and Hayley Mills. While mostly overlooked by Hollywood producers in the 1990s and early 2000s, Christie's fictions were widely enjoyed on British television, notably with *Agatha Christie's Poirot* (1989–2013), featuring David Suchet in the lead role, and *Agatha Christie's Marple* (2004–13), starring Geraldine McEwan as Miss Marple in its first three seasons, followed by Julia McKenzie from the fourth season onwards. With seventy episodes of *Agatha Christie's Poirot* and twenty-three of *Agatha Christie's Marple,* these long-running programs testify to the protean possibilities of adaptation in Christie's corpus: quite simply, such a well-stocked storehouse of source texts will likely outlast any single program's effort to adapt them all.

In more recent years, Sarah Phelps has written screenplays for several prestige adaptations of Christie's novels into television miniseries, including *And Then There Were None* (2015), *The Witness for the Prosecution* (2016), *Ordeal by Innocence* (2018), *The ABC Murders* (2018), and *The Pale Horse* (2020). Kenneth Branagh has reinvigorated the 1970s cinematic tradition of adapting Christie's novels with all-star casts, including his *Murder on the Orient Express* (2017) and *Death on the Nile* (2022), in which he cast himself as a remarkably spry Poirot. Notably, Branagh's adaptations should be seen as doubly adapted, as he must respond both to Christie's source texts and to the 1970s film adaptations of these narratives, which suggests that, while Christie's original visions continue to play an important role in retelling her tales, so too do the intervening perspectives of previous adapters. Branagh's portrayal of Poirot would likely have raised Christie's eyebrows, for he indulges in some of the thrilling derring-do of action heroes rather than solely the cerebral gymnastics of her novels. This brief overview of adaptations of Christie's corpus focuses on British and American productions, yet, as Mark Aldridge documents, the appeal of her fiction extends across the globe, with French, German, Russian, Indian, and Japanese filmmakers, among others, also translating her work to the screen.[8]

Given the impressive number of Christie adaptations over the decades, it is perhaps not surprising, though no less remarkable, that several actors and other creative talents have built their careers on the foundations of her fiction. Such a dynamic is readily apparent for the many television series, notably the eponymous performances of Hickson in *Miss Marple,* of Suchet in *Agatha Christie's Poirot,* and of McEwan and then McKenzie in *Agatha Christie's Marple.* Perhaps more surprisingly, such a dynamic is also apparent for stars of theatre and film. Charles Laughton enjoyed an early success in his distinguished career playing Poirot in the theatrical version of *Alibi*—according to a contemporary reviewer, "Mr. Laughton is a great actor, and in *Alibi* he gives a great performance"[9]—and then, almost thirty years later, he received an Academy Award nomination for his performance as Sir Wilfrid Roberts in *The Witness for the Prosecution.* Peter Ustinov tackled the role of Poirot in *Death on the Nile, Evil under the Sun,* and *Appointment with Death,* as well as in a series of television movies: *Thirteen at Dinner* (1985), *Dead Man's Folly* (1986), and *Murder in Three Acts* (1986). Angela Lansbury, who steals scenes in the supporting role of Salome Otterbourne in *Death on the Nile,* was then cast as Miss Marple for *The Mirror Crack'd* (1980), paving the way for her Christie-inspired television series *Murder, She Wrote* (1984–96)—the title of which echoes Margaret Rutherford's earlier film *Murder, She Said.* Writers have similarly benefited greatly by establishing their expertise as adapters of Christie's works, perhaps most notably Anthony Shaffer. Shaffer published and produced a number of his own works, most notably the Tony Award-winning play *Sleuth* (1970), yet over the course of his career, Christie adaptations offered a steady stream of work and remuneration, including uncredited contributions to the screenplay of *Murder on the Orient Express* and credited work for *Death on the Nile, Evil under the Sun,* and *Appointment with Death.*

Whereas certain critics have tautologically derided Christie's fiction because it adheres to the parameters of genre fiction, several films adapted from her narratives have assisted in collapsing any arbitrary distinction between genre fiction and narrative art by garnering widespread accolades. Billy Wilder's adaptation of *Witness for the Prosecution* was lauded with six Academy Award nominations: for Best Picture, Best Actor in a Leading Role (Charles Laughton), Best Actress in a Supporting Role (Elsa Lanchester), Best Director (Billy Wilder), Best Sound Recording (Gordon Sawyer), and Best Film Editing (Daniel Mandell). Despite her distaste for most adaptations of her novels, Christie effusively praised Wilder's film: "Almost everything I have seen of mine which has been done for the cinema I disliked intensely. The only one that I really enjoyed was *Witness for the Prosecution,* which was done in America, I think by Billy Wilder."[10] Many critics would also select Lumet's *Murder on the Orient Express* as one of the finest adaptations of a Christie novel. Like *Witness for the Prosecution,* it garnered six Academy Award Nominations, including Best Actor (Albert Finney), Best Adapted Screenplay, Best Cinematography, Best Costume

Design, and Best Original Score; Ingrid Bergman won her third Oscar for her supporting role. While not receiving as much widespread critical acclaim, John Guillermin's *Death on the Nile* (1978) won the Academy Award for Best Costume Design. Collectively, these critically praised adaptations of Christie's novels raise the question: How bad can a novel be if a film adapted from it wins critical acclaim?

As much as Christie's fiction has been adapted into other media, so has her life story inspired a range of works. In effect, she has metamorphosed from a historical human being into a narrative character bearing only a fluctuating sense of any biographical reality. Kathleen Tynan fictionalized the circumstances of Christie's mysterious 1926 disappearance in *Agatha;* this novel was itself adapted into a 1979 film directed by Michael Apted and starring Vanessa Redgrave as Agatha and Timothy Dalton as Archie Christie. Sam McCarver includes Christie in his novel *The Case of Compartment 7,* and as much as he outlines the research undertaken to accurately transform the human author into a fictional character, the resulting vision of Agatha Christie reflects his authorial needs more than it does the biographical realities of her life.[11] Tom Dalton has penned a series of alternative-history television films of Christie's life, in which the author solves murders that she encounters. In *Agatha and the Truth of Murder* (2018), *Agatha and the Curse of Ishtar* (2019), and *Agatha and the Midnight Murders* (2020), Dalton's Christie becomes the latest detective in the lineage including C. Auguste Dupin, Sherlock Holmes, Hercule Poirot, and Miss Marple—in effect, in the lineage that Christie herself helped to build. Like Tynan, Marie Benedict tackles Christie's mysterious 1926 disappearance in her novel *The Mystery of Mrs. Christie* (2021), envisioning the writer as trapping her duplicitous husband in a web of suspicion in order to compel him to exonerate her of blame for their divorce and to publicly acknowledge his adulterous affair with Nancy Neele.

Owing to the bounty of Christie adaptations and space limitations of this book, the remainder of this chapter addresses one of the quirkier entries in the canon—the 1980 version of *The Mirror Crack'd.* While many Christie adaptations faithfully adhere to her plotlines, themes, and tone, others veer markedly from their sources into more comic territory. As detailed in chapter 6, Christie's works evince her unique comic sensibilities in their debts to the comedy of manners tradition, yet *The Mirror Crack'd,* as penned by screenwriter Barry Sandler, prefers the more riotous effects of camp over her more rarefied tone. As such, it provides a compelling example of the vagaries of what we might term queer adaptation, when a gay man rewrites a straight woman's story, in which memorable effects can be achieved, even if the author herself would have likely disapproved of them. *The Mirror Crack'd* thus exemplifies a deeper paradox than simply Christie's dislike of many adaptations of her work, in the possibility that the source text can be reframed as perversely faithful to her vision.

Barry Sandler's Camp Adaptation of *The Mirror Crack'd*

With such films as *Kansas City Bomber* (1972), *Gable and Lombard* (1976), and *The Duchess and the Dirtwater Fox* (1976) to his credit, screenwriter Barry Sandler established his name in the 1970s as one of Hollywood's fresher and more prolific talents. His place in Hollywood history is assured owing to his screenplay for *Making Love* (1982), the first major studio release depicting a gay romance, and he achieved another career highlight in the 1980s with *Crimes of Passion* (1984), an erotic thriller that features Kathleen Turner and Anthony Perkins in memorably committed performances and is today recognized as one of director Ken Russell's most daring and engrossing films. Among the other milestones of his career, Sandler transformed Christie's *The Mirror Crack'd* (1980) into a campy gem through his gleefully decadent screenplay. Following the success of the 1970s blockbuster adaptations of Christie's *Murder on the Orient Express* and *Death on the Nile,* and with similar over-the-top Hollywood panache, the film adaptation of *The Mirror Crack'd* features an all-star cast, notably Angela Lansbury as Christie's beloved detective Miss Marple, along with Elizabeth Taylor, Rock Hudson, Tony Curtis, Kim Novak, and other celebrities. Director Guy Hamilton, who is best remembered for his work on the James Bond franchise, including *Goldfinger* (1964), *Diamonds Are Forever* (1971), *Live and Let Die* (1973), and *The Man with the Golden Gun* (1974), joined this talented screenwriter and these big stars. With this pedigree, *The Mirror Crack'd* promised a familiar formula of cinematic adaptation from the 1970s yet one that Sandler leavened with unexpected camp pleasures.

Within cinema's collaborative milieu, screenwriters seeking a camp effect face the challenge of achieving their humorous vision through the coordinated efforts of the director, actors, and other professionals creatively contributing to the film's production. Given these conditions, *The Mirror Crack'd* illustrates the potential and pitfalls of queer adaptation, particularly when the director's vision fails to align with the screenwriter's. Within the ambit of this chapter, the term *queer adaptation* refers to any of the variety of ways in which a source text is repurposed for another medium while highlighting the expression of transgressive desires, whether those desires are grounded in the erotic, aesthetic, or another field. In so doing, a queer adaptation might accelerate or contain the queerness depicted in its source. Acceleration and containment are exemplified respectively by Frank Perry's over-the-top staging of Christina Crawford's *Mommie Dearest* (memoir 1978; film 1981), which transmutes the horrors of child abuse into campy hysterics, and Steven Spielberg's restrained staging of Alice Walker's *The Color Purple* (novel 1982; film 1985), which cloaks the lesbianism at the novel's heart. Balancing this binary, certain queer adaptations aim for fidelity —an admittedly conflicted term in adaptation studies but one that appears appropriate for such films as James Ivory's version of E. M. Forster's *Maurice* (novel written 1913–14 and published 1971; film 1987) and Ang Lee's version of Annie Proulx's *Brokeback Mountain* (short story 1997; film 2005).

At first glance, Christie's *The Mirror Crack'd* would not appear a particularly apt vehicle for camp humor, as it follows the traditional parameters of the murder mystery, and so Sandler's rollicking adaptation belongs firmly to the accelerative mode of queer adaptation. Susan Sontag famously defined camp as "a vision of the world in terms of style—but a particular kind of style. It is the love of the exaggerated, the 'off,' of things-being-what-they-are-not."[12] She further suggests: "Camp is art that proposes itself seriously, but cannot be taken altogether seriously because it is 'too much.'"[13] Camp often begins with parody, yet as Moe Meyer proposes, "Camp emerges as specifically queer parody possessing cultural and ideological analytic potential. . . . Parody becomes the process whereby the marginalized and disenfranchised advance their own interests."[14] With this form of queer parody, camp enables artists to speak back to dominant forms of discourse, even in such genres as detective fiction that might be assumed to be escapist fare. Of key importance in understanding the ways in which camp functions in *The Mirror Crack'd* is the way in which subversive humor builds queer communities, as Philip Core argues: "Besides being a signal, camp was and remains the way in which homosexuals and other groups of people with double lives can find a *lingua franca*."[15] For screenwriters, the challenges of camp are magnified in that they can parody existing cultural artifacts and pen camp dialogue but cannot ensure camp stagings and camp performances to capture their vision. That is to say, queer screenwriters can never ensure that Hollywood's power structures—most clearly enforced by the producers bankrolling the project and the directors controlling its filming—will respect their artistic vision and instead seek to normalize any transgressive pleasures they aspire to introduce.

On his way to creating a camp gem, Sandler was confronted with a decidedly non-campy, if at times genially amusing, source text in *The Mirror Crack'd*. In Christie's novel (and with these storylines followed in the film), victim Heather Badcock dies at a reception hosted by actress Marina Gregg (Elizabeth Taylor), but investigators soon become convinced that Marina was the killer's intended target. Sidelined by the infirmities of age, Miss Marple (Angela Lansbury) relies on her nephew, Inspector Craddock (Edward Fox), to keep her apprised of the investigation's progress as he interviews the many suspects. (As Sandler avers, this stricture limits the film's narrative action: "Miss Marple can't launch an investigation; she has to do it through [Craddock's] investigation." Given these conditions, Sandler says that he was "kind of saddled with that; it's hard to make her an active heroine.") Craddock pursues his investigation by interrogating the prime suspects, including Marina's husband Jason Rudd (Rock Hudson); Jason's infatuated secretary Ella Zielinsky (Geraldine Chaplin); Marina's former romantic rival Lola Brewster (Kim Novak); and producer Ardwyck Fenn, renamed Martin N. Fenn in the film (Tony Curtis). Through her keen attention to detail and her powers of deduction, Miss Marple solves the crime. Following a chance encounter many years ago, Heather infected Marina with German measles while she was pregnant, resulting in her child being born with severe intellectual disabilities. Stunned to meet the woman who precipitated such emotional agony, Marina poisons her own drink, surreptitiously jogs Heather's elbow, and then insists that Heather take her drink, with the victim expiring soon after.

The film version of *The Mirror Crack'd* adheres to the basic trajectory of Christie's plot, which, as Sandler declares, was required by the film's licensing agreement: "according to the terms of the Christie estate, you had to stick to the exact plot; you couldn't change the killer or suspects." Expanding on this point, Sandler mentions the filmmakers were granted a degree of artistic license in that they "could create new dialogue and conflicts, [and] could change settings."[16] Along with any such contractual requirements, cinematic adaptations frequently must streamline their source narrative due to film's standard temporal parameters of roughly ninety minutes to two hours. In light of these constraints, several peripheral characters were omitted, including Miss Knight, Miss Marple's officious and annoying companion assisting her during her convalescence; Arthur Badcock, Heather Badcock's husband and Marina Gregg's first husband; Hailey Preston, Jason Rudd's assistant; and Dr. Gilchrist, Marina's physician. Margot Bence remains in the film as the photographer who captures the shot of Marina standing frozen while Heather Badcock prattles but loses her status as a suspect. The plotline concerning Marina's adopted and then abandoned children, of whom Margot is one, is mentioned briefly yet remains undeveloped as a potential motive. Numerous other minor changes could be mentioned, but more significant than any shift in the plotline is Sandler's campy shift in tone and dialogue, resulting in a film illustrating the humorous possibilities of queer adaptation.

Comedy provides a critical means for screenwriters to energize the pacing of a murder mystery that might otherwise consist mainly of a series of interviews. As Philip Jenkinson notes: "[many] Agatha Christie adaptations have attempted to up-date their material with humour."[17] *Death on the Nile* illustrates this practice, with Christie's novel enlivened by Bette Davis and Maggie Smith's petty bickering in their roles as Mrs. Van Schuyler and Miss Bowers, not to mention the image of young Egyptian boys mooning Bette Davis / Mrs. Van Schuyler as she serenely sits on the boat's deck observing the view. At the same time, the interjection of humor into a murder mystery can undercut its rising tension, and some adaptations of Christie's works have been snubbed for attempting this admixture of tones, such as in Wolcott Gibbs's review of the theatrical adaptation of *And Then There Were None:* "the humor that has been inserted is always broad and often has a tendency to defeat the author's sinister intent."[18]

Christie infuses *The Mirror Crack'd* with several moments of wry humor, in a manner consistent with her interest in the comedy of manners tradition. The culture clash between the rural residents of St. Mary Mead and the cosmopolitan filmmakers establishes an underlying comic tenor to the novel, as do Miss Marple's skirmishes with her companion Miss Knight, such as when the latter suggests that she will make Miss Marple a "nice eggnog" and pedantically prompts, "We'd like that, wouldn't we?" Miss Marple demurely replies with sweet yet arch irony: "I don't know whether *you* would like it. . . . *I* should be delighted for you to have it if you would like it" (168; italics in the original). This central ingredient of humor in the Christie canon, both in its literary and cinematic incarnations, was notably absent in the first draft of the screenplay for *The Mirror Crack'd,* which was penned by British writer Jonathan Hales. Hales achieved notable success in the 1970s with such television programs as *Manhunt* and *The Guardians;* his most commercial triumph came later in his career with *Star Wars: Episode 2—Attack of the Clones* (2002). As is common with Hollywood screenwriting, although Hales and Sandler share a screen credit, they did not collaborate on the project. Sandler explains: "The script wasn't quite working," and so "the producers wanted an American writer to modernize it." He further observes: "Hales's script was very British, and the Americans were subsidiary characters. They had no life, no color, and so I wanted to give it a bitchier sensibility. The producers said, 'Great! Go for it!'" And go for it, he did, with great gusto.

Although Christie's humor does not fall within the purview of camp, nor does the humor of most of the adaptations of her work, she evinces a keen interest in theatricality, with the exaggerations of this trope conducive to camp humor. R. A. York comments: "Theatricality is in fact one of the basic concerns and one of the basic mechanisms of the Christie novels," noting further that "many of the central characters in her novels are professional actors."[19] Because they are adept at assuming roles and feigning emotions, actors frequently appear as suspects in Christie's cast of characters, and her murderers must by necessity hone their skills in dissembling—until they are revealed as the killers. Significantly, many of Christie's actors appear as larger-than-life figures who claim the attention of all bystanders through their sheer magnetism, such as in the description of the victim of *Murder in Mesopotamia:* "Mrs. Leidner was a bit of a film star in private life. She *had* to be the center of things—in the limelight" (118–19). In *Evil Under the Sun,* Arlena Stuart Marshall similarly stuns the attention of all onlookers: "Her arrival had all the importance of a stage entrance. Moreover, she walked as though she knew it" (10); another character comments of her, "It's IT, my boy . . . That's what it is—IT" (12), referring to that ineffable feature of charismatic celebrity. With a formulation readily applicable to Marina Gregg, Merja Makinen affirms: "The type of the Hollywood actress comes to stand for self-absorbed egotism in Christie's work."[20] "Self-absorbed egotism" is also the hallmark of divas and drag queens in the exaggerated theatricality that stands as camp's hallmark. This is not to suggest that Sandler transforms Elizabeth Taylor into a drag queen in her role—although the excessive performance of gender allows such a reading—but that he exploited the big egos and bigger insecurities rampant in the entertainment industry for the deep humor of shallow behavior.

In accentuating Christie's interest in Hollywood, film, and performativity throughout *The Mirror Crack'd,* Sandler highlights recurring themes in Christie's corpus, which he further imbues with camp humor. The film begins with a parody of the murder mystery genre, both in its novelistic and cinematic incarnations, in order simultaneously to pay homage to and to subvert the genre's foundations. A story filmed in black and white unfolds on the screen, with the establishing shot of an English manor house accompanied by the sound of thunder cracking to create the effect of a (clichéd) "dark and stormy night." As the camera moves inside, viewers observe the (clichéd) butler greeting the (clichéd) detective clad in a (clichéd and obviously inspired by Sherlock Holmes) tweed coat. The detective enters the drawing room and (clichéd) dialogue ensues. Mr. Montrose, one of the suspects in the murder of Lord Fenley, protests, "Inspector, you're not trying to imply that one of us could have actually performed such a loathsome deed?" to which the Inspector gravely replies, "Not only do I believe it, Mr. Montrose, but I have the evidence to prove it. All of you had sufficient motive. It could have been . . . any one of you." The Inspector then expostulates at length upon the various suspects and their potential (and convoluted) motives for the murder as he leads up to this scene's final cliché: the grand reveal of the murderer's identity. "Very well, then," the Inspector declares, "Lord Fenley's murderer . . ." A broken projector ends this film within a film, and it is here that the purposeful clichés of *The Mirror Crack'd* end as well. This film that viewers might have presumed they are watching is revealed to be a macguffin, a distraction entitled *Murder at Midnight* rather than the titular film itself and one that Miss Marple breezily solves for her fellow audience members. As Sandler details, "the opening scene establishes Marple as the heroine," for she sees through the tropes of the mystery genre that Sandler exposes so that he may then supersede them as the film progresses. Later in the film, Jason Rudd tells Inspector Craddock, "You've been seeing too many Charlie Chan movies, Inspector"—another sure sign that Sandler knows the tropes of the murder mystery genre and deploys them atypically and, ultimately, to camp ends.

A key trope of camp humor is simultaneously to revel in and to strip away the facades of art and performance. As Richard Dyer suggests: "Camp, by drawing attention to the artifices employed by artists, can constantly remind us that what we are seeing is only a view of life. This doesn't stop us enjoying it, but it does stop us believing too readily everything we are shown."[21] In Christie's *The Mirror Crack'd*, readers are informed of Marina's and Lola's shared occupation as actresses, but the novel does not thematize the artifice of performance to take advantage of the duplicities arising from their rivalry. In contrast, Sandler sets much of the film directly in the cinematic world better to exploit the humor of Hollywood egos invading the small English village of St. Mary Mead. Sandler's Miss Marple echoes Dyer's viewpoint in her assessment of the cinematic world: "I read not too long ago about Hollywood: 'Underneath all that phony tinsel lies the real tinsel.'" Her words provide a suitable theme for the film as a whole, for Sandler creates the film's "real tinsel"—its humor—underneath the standard plotline of a Christie mystery novel. This delight in artifice emerges as well in various characters' constructions of themselves for public consumption. When producer Martin N. Fenn is asked what his middle initial stands for, he puffily replies: "I'll tell you what it stands for. Nothing. But it sure looks great on that big silver screen, doesn't it?" In a camp world, artifice is the only reality that matters.

Camp pleasures abound in the pitched battles between Marina and Lola, a plot point that supplies the film version of *The Mirror Crack'd* with its wittiest, bitchiest dialogue. While forcing smiles for a photographer, the two actresses spar, with Marina drawing first blood: "What are you supposed to be, a birthday cake? Too bad everybody's had a piece." As the photographer requests, "Can we have a big smile, ladies?" Lola obliges, as she also coolly counterattacks: "Chin up, darling. Both of them." The photographer then encourages the women, "A little bit closer, please, ladies," and Marina prepares her enemy for the coup de grace: "Lola, dear, you know there really are only two things I dislike about you." Taking the bait, Lola queries, "Really? What are they?" Marina graciously snarls: "Your face." Wearing big hats, standing in contrasting costuming of pink and purple, and plastering on wearied smiles, Taylor and Novak play their catfight with steely determination and cutting humor (see figure 1). As Sandler recalls, although Taylor and Novak did not share any longstanding animosity, a slight professional rivalry arose over staging because Novak expressed concerned that Taylor was receiving more flattering framing from the key lighting. The director of photography assuaged Novak's concerns, consoling her that Taylor "needs it more than you do." While such a behind-the-scenes anecdote may appear inconsequential to a reading of the resulting film, it highlights the Hollywood duplicities and humor that Sandler sought to bring to the screen. In many ways, Hollywood cannot help but be camp.

*Kim Novak and Elizabeth Taylor smile for the cameras while
exchanging cutting insults, with the duality between surface
expression and actual sentiment creating a masterful camp staging.*

Within Sandler's camp reimagining of the characters, it is not only Marina
and Lola who are reimagined as bitchy divas. Ella Zielinsky stands as a rather
unremarkable character in Christie's novel, with her primary narrative purpose
emerging when she is murdered for blackmailing the killer. In Sandler's hands,
Ella blossoms through the addition of her biting, acerbic commentary on the
Hollywood divas surrounding her. Commenting on Marina's overuse of sleeping pills, she dryly declares, "You shake her, she rattles." Upon observing the impending conflict between Marina and Lola, she resignedly sighs: "Uh-oh. Mary
Queen of Sluts and Baby Bernhardt under the same roof. That's all we need."
When discussing these actresses with producer Marty Fenn, she pointedly reminds him of their mutual enmity: "Remember, they used to grind glass in each
other's cold cream." Her assessment of Fenn likewise reveals a woman exhausted
by the duplicities of her workplace—"Marty Fenn is a producer. He only lies
when he speaks"—yet capable of transmuting the dross of others' egotism into
comic pleasures.

Camp, a larger-than-life style, benefits from larger-than-life performances.
In short, the true camp artist is the biggest ham, and the script of *The Mirror
Crack'd* offers its stars numerous opportunities to exaggerate their characters
into campy caricatures. In an appropriately over-the-top performance, Tony
Curtis delivers such memorable lines as "Of course I'm a bastard. I'm the producer!" When the local vicar, bewildered by the intricacies of filmmaking, wonders aloud, "But who chooses the leading lady?" Curtis deadpans, "Whoever's
sleeping with her." He also generously offers to demystify the cinematic world
for the vicar: "What would you like to know, Vicar, baby?" In her performance
as Lola Brewster, Kim Novak plays the egomaniacal diva, virtually puffing up in
each scene to accentuate the character's excessive glamour and unbridled ego.

Concerned about her hairstyle for the film, Fenn reminds her, "Queen Elizabeth was bald," to which she snappily replies, "Not in this movie, she ain't." She snipes at Jason Rudd's last directorial effort: "I could eat a can of Kodak and puke a better movie." Great actors must avoid degrading their performances into emoting, but great camp actors indulge the pleasure of tossing out nuance in favor of exaggeration.

In his adaptation of Christie's murder mystery, Sandler faced the challenge of balancing between her interest in crime and his interest in camp, lest the crime be lost altogether. And so whereas Curtis and Novak can indulge in the campy excess of their supporting characters, Elizabeth Taylor cannot aim solely for humor in her performance as Marina Gregg because this character fears for her life—or at least she must pretend to do so. As explored above, Marina's sparring with Lola allows her to exaggeratedly enact the bitchiness of the grande dame, yet she also displays the emotional fatigue of stardom, as evidenced in her resigned doggerel while looking in the mirror and regretting the inexorable march of time: "Bags, bags, go away / Come right back on Doris Day." Sandler recalls his trepidation that Taylor might take umbrage at his humor at Marina's expense and apologized to her—"I hope you aren't too upset with some of the jokes I wrote." Taylor's reply—"They'll love me for them!"—indicates that she understood the camp appeal of his words and her performance. It is intriguing to ponder, as well, whom Taylor might have intended with her pronoun "they." Surely she is referring to her audience, but it seems at least plausible, given Taylor's longstanding support of the gay community, that she realized the camp appeal of her performance and the ways in which her gay fans both identified with and adored her. Sandler states as well that Taylor "was the only actor who said every line exactly as written"—a testament to her commitment to her performance even when the jokes at Marina's expense also reflect Taylor's metamorphosis from her youth of stunning beauty to her middle-aged years of a more Rubenesque stature. Stars are separate from their roles, except not really, for a star must be appropriate for her roles, and thus the overlap between the star and her roles that builds her star persona. One can trace the erosion of Taylor's beauty from her lead role in *Cleopatra* in 1963 to Marina Gregg in 1980, but this latter performance evidences as well her gracious and humorous resignation to time's inevitable march. Further imbuing his film with camp tropes, Sandler here plays on the "aging diva phenomenon"—a character type most memorable in Gloria Swanson's performance in *Sunset Boulevard* (1950)—but rather than rejecting the excess of such a role, Taylor embraced it.[22]

Further in his characterization of Marina, Sandler portrays her as a woman so immersed in the world of filmmaking that the other characters (and thus viewers as well) must discern whether she is reacting honestly to the dire circumstances surrounding her or merely playing her part. In this light, the doubleness of "playing a part," both for the screenwriter who writes the role and the actor who enacts it, offers another avenue for camp adaptation. This aspect of Marina's character surfaces during her interview with Inspector Craddock when Taylor's performance verges on hysteria and the hysterical: "Oh, God! It was me, wasn't it? It was me they were trying to poison, wasn't it? Who am I kidding? Somebody is trying to kill me, aren't they? Somebody is trying to . . . poison me, aren't they? Somebody is trying to kill me, aren't they? Aren't they? I know it! I can . . ." As Marina is apparently building up to an emotional breakdown, Craddock interrupts her, continuing her performance—"'I can feel it. I can almost hear them coming'"—as he then identifies the source of her words: "*Danger in the Dark*. MGM, 1932." A character always ready for the cameras, Marina lives as if on stage, which highlights the ways in which performance permeates the film as a mode of existence. The actors of this film act, as of course they must, but the characters that they play indulge in hyperbolic acting as well, thus multiplying the film's camp effect. To some degree, Sandler modeled Craddock on himself interacting with the stars on set, mentioning that he would "quote a line from one of [Taylor's] movies and see if she could get them."[23] Implicitly rebutting such critical bromides as "the death of the author," Sandler demonstrates the ways in which the author can insert himself both through the screenplay he writes and through his comic mode of interacting with the performers.

With its humorous touches, even the film's pointedly dry moments advance its overarching camp. At Marina Gregg's reception, the camera appears to bypass various townspeople when moving to or following more central characters, yet the audience hears snippets of their conversation that are virtually shocking in their stultifying banality. One villager says, "I told you I lost my borage last year in the frost?" to which his interlocutor replies, "I'm sorry about that. You know what to do, don't you? Cut it right down to the ground." In another deadening exchange, a villager states, apropos of little, "Your dear wife had a cat." His companion complains, "Yes, but it always suffered from eczema," to which the first speaker proposes, "Carrots. Mashed carrots and a little warm milk work wonders." With this eczema-afflicted cat, the film satirizes the deadening ennui of cocktail conversation, leaving viewers amused by the inanity of small talk and eager for the campy characters to seize control of the scene.

As camp offers screenwriters endless potential to queer an adaptation, such a vision must be endorsed by the director if it is to succeed, and any such contrast in artistic visions threatens to constrain the humor unleashed in the screenplay. *The Mirror Crack'd* delights with its bitchy camp, yet it is regrettable that Hamilton did not more fully accommodate Sandler's comic vision. Sandler says of Hamilton: "He was not what you would call a sensitive, woman's director; he was stern, British, and he didn't have a lot of humor." Explanding on such points, Sandler added, "I don't think he's a comedy director. He signed up for an

Agatha Christie mystery, but I turned it into a campy backstage comedy." Disappointingly, Hamilton rejected some of Sandler's more daring comic touches. As much as Novak triumphs in her performance as Lola Brewster, Sandler advocated casting Debbie Reynolds to elevate the tension between the stars and their roles, owing to the obvious overlap between Christie's plotline concerning Marina's marriages and Taylor's life when she married Eddie Fisher after he left Reynolds for her. For a bit of physical humor alluding to Taylor's recent weight gain, Sandler wanted Marina to join Jason Rudd / Hudson in bed only for it to collapse; as he tersely summarizes of this idea: "didn't happen." In a scene cut from the film, Marina runs panicked from the set after drinking her purportedly poisoned tea; Novak's Lola files her nails and deadpans: "Huh! You'd think she just spotted her diet doctor!" According to Sandler, Hamilton thought this joke dissipated the tension of the moment and he wanted to play the scene for its suspense rather than for its comedy. Mystery and comedy can be successfully merged—*The Thin Man* films provide examples—but it is also a challenge to unite disparate narrative modes, with one seeking to build suspense and the other seeking to release cathartic laughter. In this instance, Hamilton opted for mystery over camp, only to find that, in the final analysis, Sandler's camp humor made the film immeasurably more memorable.

Although it is now heralded as a camp classic, several contemporary reviewers of *The Mirror Crack'd* apparently could not see the joke. The *Newsweek* reviewer derided it as a "starchy effort that is not only set in 1952 but appears to have been made then," denouncing in particular "Guy Hamilton's mothball-scented direction."[24] The *New York* reviewer declared, "Every poky, pawky Christie crotchet—so delightful to the true fan—has been reverently preserved, but Hamilton can't find a style for the fussiness that would make it witty. It's a stupefyingly methodical movie."[25] *Maclean's* dismissed the film for its leisurely tempo: "Poorly lit, hastily edited and paced like a particularly boring game of Clue, the movie has the feel of a parish hall and the vitality of a vicar."[26] With similar terms, Rex Reed, writing for *Vogue,* sniped: "If anything creaks, it's not the doors of the inner sanctum, it's the direction of Guy Hamilton. This is a slow, soft little film with an annoying lack of pace."[27] From these opinions, it would appear that *The Mirror Crack'd* should have quickly faded into obscurity, a footnote to film history memorable only as a regrettable effort in the otherwise stellar cinematographies of Taylor, Lansbury, and Hudson.

Camp films, however, must be assessed through camp hermeneutics rather than through a standard critical lens, and a quick overview of camp classics demonstrates that such disparaging reviews are disappointingly predictable, as few mainstream reviewers appreciate or even recognize camp. Classics of the form, including *Beat the Devil* (dir. John Huston, 1953), *Suddenly Last Summer* (dir. Joseph L. Mankiewicz, 1959), *The Rocky Horror Picture Show* (dir.

Jim Sharman, 1975), and *Showgirls* (dir. Paul Verhoeven, 1995), to name only a few, have been critically dismissed only for audiences more receptive to their pleasures to find them as the years pass. Several of the more positive reviews of *The Mirror Crack'd* praised Sandler's campy script while assailing its stilted direction, thus foreshadowing such a shift in its critical reception. In this regard, the *Time* reviewer came closest to the mark, noting that "the good lines make *Mirror* more fun to watch than it has any right to be."[28] The *Maclean's* reviewer acknowledged that "the very idea of Liz Taylor and Kim Novak playing the Queen of Scots and Elizabeth R is a source of endless amusement, and the [screenwriter has] provided a spectacularly bitchy interplay for these two."[29] Rex Reed leavens his criticism: "When Novak looks in the mirror, rips off her wig, and yells 'Comb it out—you might find Amelia Earhart,' . . . you don't have to ask who steals the movie or why the mirror cracked."[30] Even the grumpy *Newsweek* reviewer conceded that the film's "bitchy fireworks are . . . the most arresting moments in this latest all-star Agatha Christie entry."[31]

Certainly, the film's enduring popularity, as evidenced by the enthusiastic reception it received at a January 2017 screening hosted by Outfest in West Hollywood and its recent rerelease on Blu-Ray DVD, testifies both that critics and audiences often seek divergent pleasures from the screen and that the film has withstood the test of time, particularly for queer audiences. In a recent assessment of Novak's career singling out *The Mirror Crack'd*, Liz Smith states simply, "Every line is classic."[32] Campy pleasures blossom in the margins for resistant viewers who reject the standard trajectories and tropes of narrative and instead appreciate a humor that bends askew yet, for those in the know, never fails to hit its mark. For these reasons, *The Mirror Crack'd* has secured a beloved position in the queer film canon of camp, even though Christie herself paid relatively little attention to queer culture in her works. Few gay characters enter her pages, and as R. A. York proposes, "she shows simple distaste for male homosexuals" in her depictions of them.[33] (In *The Mirror Crack'd*, a minor character is disparaged as a "pansy" [164], in a mostly unremarkable yet telling example of Christie's depiction of gay men.) Yet camp's power as a comic mode allows it to circulate subversively where one might least expect it—in *The Mirror Crack'd*, a puzzling murder mystery featuring the keen-witted Miss Marple snaps to life in Sandler's queer and campy adaptation. And despite the disjunction between Sandler's and Christie's styles, he also worked on the 1982 adaptation of her *Evil Under the Sun*—although the credits show only Anthony Shaffer as the screenwriter— and her *And Then There Were None* inspired the basic narrative structure of his *Knock 'Em Dead* (2014). Agatha Christie's novels may not spring to mind as a wellspring of camp comedy, but Sandler has proved the queer compatibility of her murders and his bitchy humor.

As *The Mirror Crack'd* exemplifies, adaptations should not be judged as much by their fidelity to their source texts but more by their unique perspectives on them. The stronger entries in the canon of Christie adaptations—Wilder's *Witness for the Prosecution,* Lumet's *Murder on the Orient Express,* Hamilton's *The Mirror Crack'd,* Phelps's many television miniseries—are united primarily by their reliance on a Christie source text but then diverge notably in their tones, styles, moods, and atmosphere. Looking to the future, Christie's vast corpus promises to continually challenge authors and dramatists, screenwriters and directors, and a variety of other creative talents to reframe her fictional universe for new audiences, including video games designers, as several titles have been adopted in this format. In each instance, a Christie source text will serve to inspire, but it remains in the hands of the adapters whether her works will succeed in their latest retellings, in whichever medium they may be reframed. Christie need not have appreciated the vast majority of adaptations of her work, might not have even found a given adaptation a recognizable version of her story, but, in this great paradox of her legacy, she continues to benefit mightily from them, decades after her death.

Conclusion

Literary Criticism and the Mystery of
Christie's Murderous Pleasures

Agatha Christie and Max Mallowan undoubtedly saw eye-to-eye on many issues during the course of their long marriage, and given their words on the subject of literary criticism, one can safely assume that they would agree on the futility of this book. Christie opined: "I write books which are meant to entertain people, and to sell for that reason. I have never seen any point in informal studies of an author's work."[1] Mallowan, adopting a franker tone, asserted: "I have the feeling, unfair perhaps, that the analytical critic of detective fiction is either a knave or a fool."[2] As I reread all of Christie's fiction to write this volume, one of Poirot's chance remarks seemed to be speaking directly, although I hope ironically, to me: "Imbeciles are writing the lives of other imbeciles every day. It is, as you say, done" (*Poirot Loses a Client*, 73). While the entire point of this volume is to argue that Christie should not be dismissed as an unsophisticated writer, the quotation's deeper relevance to this project and my efforts satirically hit home. Such a viewpoint is expressed more compassionately by Mark Easterbrook, the protagonist of *The Pale Horse:* "I had suffered from one of those sudden revulsions that all writers know. . . . What did they matter? Why did I want to write about them?" (4). A book's conclusion is hardly the place for solipsistic navel-gazing about the dignity—or indignity—of one's efforts, but Christie's and Mallowan's viewpoints encapsulate the fundamental challenge of literary criticism, with Christie's characters capturing many authors' underlying apprehension of the ultimate futility of such arduous efforts.

For all that I have attempted to posit reasons behind Christie's extraordinary success and the lasting appeal of her novels by examining seven central paradoxes of her corpus, and in doing so sought to contextualize what others have criticized in her fiction, Hercule Poirot's comments on Ariadne Oliver's fiction apparently capture Christie's assessment of her own work: "I do not wholly approve of her works, mind you. The happenings in them are highly improbable. The long arm of coincidence is far too freely employed. And, being young at the time, she was foolish enough to make her detective a Finn, and it is clear that she knows nothing about Finns or Finland except possibly the works of Sibelius. Still, she has an original habit of mind, she makes an occasional shrewd deduction, and of later years she has learnt a good deal about things about which she did not know before" (*Clocks*, 109–10). These words were published in 1963, amid the final third of Christie's career, and they likely represent her astute and unapologetic assessment of her strengths and weaknesses. Yes, improbable events and coincidences often advance her killers' efforts, which are sometimes counterbalanced by equally improbable revelations of their guilt, even while her novels stand as striking original works in which the clues have been laid carefully and cunningly and her prose irresistibly edges readers along from beginning to end.

As many critics have disparaged Christie's fiction as substandard literary fare, surely many will similarly dismiss this volume's efforts to contextualize her achievements. The paradoxes collectively outlined in these pages—the autobiographical elements of her novels despite her reclusive persona, her inclusion in the pantheon of the Golden Age of Detective Fiction while ignoring her peers' protocols for the genre, her status as "Queen of the Cozies" despite her often stark and occasionally hardboiled themes, her literary interests as refracted through the codes of genre fiction, her alternating and intermingling of comic and tragic themes, her simultaneous endorsement and critique of English insularity, and her disdain for adaptations that boosted her success—point to but cannot fully capture the mercurial reasons why so many readers continue to find her books virtually addictive, as many fans report a period of their life, whether in adolescence or adulthood, when they consumed as many of them as they could find. These paradoxes illuminate but cannot define Christie fully, and other readers have posited additional striking paradoxes in her literature and its reception, such as in Sophie Hannah's perceptive question: "How are her books able to be, simultaneously, simple enough that 12-year-olds can love them, yet complex enough to pose an impossible challenge to a bright adult mind?"[3]

On a concluding note relevant both to the reception of Agatha Christie's fiction and the efforts of *Understanding Agatha Christie,* perhaps literary criticism should unite its focus on the amorphously defined realm of aesthetics to concentrate equally on the more widely experienced field of *pleasure.* Critics may never agree on whether Christie's novels succeed aesthetically—although I hope the discussions of the poetic, comic, and tragic elements of her fiction have advanced a defense of her on aesthetic lines—but surely all must concede that they have brought untold pleasure to millions and millions of readers. Literature should provide a realm of enjoyment as well of beauty. George Orwell posited of genre fiction: "All one can say is that, while civilization remains such that one needs distraction from time to time, 'light' literature has its appointed place; also that there is such a thing as sheer skill, or native grace, which may have more survival value than erudition or intellectual power."[4] In some instances, the "light" eclipses the "heavy," and, even if one considers Christie's work only as genre fiction and overlooks her more challenging themes and her literary achievements, it is nonetheless wondrous to consider her durable appeal, her books' lasting pleasures, for so many readers. Surely there is no paradox, no mystery, in that.

NOTES

ONE: Understanding Agatha Christie

1. Christie, *Autobiography,* 344.

2. Chandler, quoted in Sophia Hannah, "No One Should Condescend to Agatha Christie."

3. James, *Talking about Detective Fiction,* 97–98.

4. Nabokov, quoted in Israel Shenker, "The Past Master of Mysteries."

5. Sandbrook, "Clever-clogs Critics."

6. Symons, *Bloody Murder,* 137.

7. Moon, "Agatha Christie," 72.

8. Grossvogel, "Agatha Christie," 265.

9. Kenney, "Detecting a Novel Use," 127.

10. "New Mystery Stories," BR25.

11. "Books: Murder Market," 67.

12. Irvin, "New Mystery Stories," 122.

13. Neimark, "Human Nature Is the Culprit," BR49.

14. Trewin, "Mixed Weather," 482.

15. Barnard, *A Talent to Deceive,* 123–24.

16. Mallowan, *Mallowan's Memoirs,* 211.

17. Gill, *Agatha Christie,* 7.

18. Cawelti, *Adventure, Mystery, and Romance,* 119.

19. The enduring and combustible issue of who determines which books belong to the literary canon—and whether such a canon exists—cannot be more than acknowledged here, but in suggesting that Wells, Verne, Shelley, Stoker, Poe, and Green have achieved the status of canonical authors, I refer to their inclusion in the Penguin Classics series. Indeed, it seems probable that several of Christie's novels will join this list when the copyrights of her books expire.

20. Updike, "Agatha Christie and Beatrix Potter," 52.

TWO: Agatha Christie's Life and Puzzling Persona

1. In this chapter, I cite the following sources parenthetically: Agatha Christie's *Autobiography* and *Come Tell Me How You Live,* Max Mallowan's *Mallowan's Memoirs,* Willa

Petschek's "Agatha Christie," and Laura Thompson's *Agatha Christie*. To avoid confusion and redundancy, Agatha Christie and members of her family are referred to by their first names.

2. "Keeping Posted," 108.

3. Grant, "A Tribute to Agatha Christie," 106.

4. "15,000 Hunt Vainly for Mrs. Christie," 1.

5. "Mrs. Christie Has Lost Memory," 4.

6. "Mrs. Christie Has Lost Memory," 4.

7. *And Then There Were None* was originally titled *Ten Little N------*, and it was also published as *Ten Little Indians*. Throughout this volume, I use the title *And Then There Were None* and phrase sentences to avoid using the original title while retaining an accurate account of Christie's career.

8. Plain, "'Tale Engineering,'" 180.

9. Green, *Curtain Up*, 1.

10. Agatha Christie, Introduction to Peter Saunder's *The Mousetrap Man*, 7.

11. Tyler, "Curtains for Poirot," 24.

12. Kingston, "The Ultimate Whodunit," 45.

13. Spenser, *The Faerie Queene*, book 1, canto 40, lines 9–10.

14. Mochrie, "They Make Crime Pay," 28.

15. Dyer, *Stars*, 22.

16. Redmond, *Celebrity*, 3.

17. Mathew Prichard, quoted in Green, *Curtain Up*, v; italics in the original.

18. Mathew Prichard, quoted in Culhane, "The Woman with a Knack for Murder," 95.

19. Norman, *Agatha Christie*, 158.

20. Yiannitsaros, "'Tea and scandal at four-thirty,'" 78.

21. "Mistress of Mystery," 69.

22. Agatha Christie, quoted in "The Talk of the Town," 24.

23. Rowse, *Memories*, 90 and 103.

24. "Mme. Whodunit," 13.

25. Bernthal, "'If not yourself, who would you be?'"

26. Birns and Birns, "Detective Fiction and the Prose of Everyday Life," 219.

27. Curran, *Agatha Christie's Secret Notebooks*, 101; see also Curran's *Agatha Christie: Murder in the Making*.

THREE: The Scofflaw of the Golden Age of Detective Fiction

1. Poe, *Collected Tales*, 141; italics in the original.

2. Gaboriau, *The Widow Lerouge*, 270.

3. Christie, "Agatha Christie on Mystery Fiction," 27–28.

4. In "The Boscombe Valley Mystery" and "The Adventure of the Crooked Man," Holmes says instead, "You know my method" and "You know my methods, Watson" (Doyle, *Complete Sherlock Holmes*, vol. 2, 214 and 416).

5. As Holmes explains to Watson, "I had grasped the significance of the silence of the dog, for one true inference invariably suggests others. . . . Obviously the midnight

visitor was someone whom the dog knew well" (Doyle, *Complete Sherlock Holmes,* vol. 2, 349).

6. Christie, "Agatha Christie on Mystery Fiction," 28.

7. Barnard, *A Talent to Deceive,* 206.

8. Green, *The Leavenworth Case,* 10 and 305–6.

9. Carr, *The Hollow Man,* 103.

10. Petschek, "Agatha Christie," 130.

11. Petschek, "Agatha Christie," 129.

12. Chesterton, "A Defence of Detective Stories," 3–4.

13. Strachey, "The Golden Age of English Detection," 12–13.

14. Stern, "The Case of the Corpse in the Blind Alley," 233.

15. Wilson, *Classics and Commercials,* 234 and 263.

16. Freeman, "The Art of the Detective Story," 9.

17. In a vast number of detective novels of this era, Chinese and other Asian characters, including Anglo-Asian and American-Asian characters. were routinely depicted as murderously nefarious. Knox's rule alludes to the ubiquity of this trope and condemns it for its obviousness. Earl Derr Biggers's Charlie Chan, a Honolulu detective, also rebuts the simplistic characterization of Asian characters as suspicious, although other regressive tropes remain in his portrayal of his protagonist. Knox's rule and Biggers's Charlie Chan implicitly condemn the widely known figure of Dr. Fu Manchu, the villainous mastermind of many of Sax Rohmer's novels.

18. Knox, "A Detective Story Decalogue," 194–96.

19. Van Dine, "S. S. Van Dine Sets Down," 129–31.

20. Constitution and Rules of the Detection Club, reproduced in Edwards, *The Golden Age of Murder,* appendix 1.

21. "The Detection Club Oath," 198.

22. Queen, *The Siamese Twin Mystery,* 134.

23. Carr, *The Hollow Man,* 151–52.

24. Makinen, "Contradicting the Golden Age," 85.

25. Van Dine, "S. S. Van Dine Sets Down," 131.

26. Faktorovich, *The Formulas of Popular Fiction,* 13.

27. Knight, *Secrets of Crime Fiction Classics,* 13–32.

FOUR: The Hardboiled Queen of the Cozies

1. Leitch, "Wanted: A New Theory of the Cozy," 78. For an example of Christie's title as "Queen of the Cozies," see Mundow, *"Agatha Christie Review,"* C5.

2. Grant, "A Tribute to Agatha Christie," 106.

3. Penzler, quoted in Fryxell, "All about Agatha," 44.

4. Stasio, "Murder Least Foul," BR42.

5. "The Escape of Agatha Christie," 38.

6. O'Brien, *Hardboiled America,* 16.

7. Leitch, "Wanted: A New Theory of the Cozy," 78.

8. Heissenbüttel, "Rules of the Game of the Crime Novel," 80.

9. Delamater and Prigozy, *The Detective in American Fiction, Film, and Television,* preface (n.p.).

10. Rowland, "Cooking the Books," 158; italics in the original.

11. G. M. Malliet, quoted in Cogdill, "Birth of a Cozy Writer," 24.

12. Madden, "Anne Riordan," 3.

13. *Poirot Loses a Client,* also published as *Dumb Witness,* includes a less apparent example of this trope: although these titles do not allude to the nursery rhyme "Mary, Mary, Quite Contrary," the novel's plot matches that of "How Does Your Garden Grow?" one of the short stories of *The Regatta Mystery.*

14. Christie also alludes to the Charles Bravo poisoning in *Ordeal by Innocence,* 69, and *Elephants Can Remember,* 55.

15. Powers, *True Crime Parallels,* 132.

16. Powers, *True Crime Parallels,* 1; italics in original. On Christie and true crime, see also Holgate, *Stranger Than Fiction.*

17. Acocella, "Queen of Crime," 82.

18. Yang, "Psychoanalysis and Detective Fiction," 596–97.

19. Cain, Preface to *The Butterfly,* ix; italics in original.

FIVE: The Poet of Genre Fiction

1. Agatha Christie, quoted in Rowse, *Memories,* 88.

2. "The Mallowans," 52.

3. Sayers, quoted in Chandler, "The Simple Art of Murder," 231.

4. Holquist, "Murder She Says," 27.

5. Cawelti, *Adventure, Mystery, and Romance,* 13.

6. Gelder, *Popular Fiction,* 35–39.

7. Ewers, "Genre in Transit," 97.

8. Humble, *The Feminine Middlebrow Novel,* 11 and 53.

9. Lecercle, "Three Accounts of Literary Style," 159.

10. Holquist, "Murder She Says," 28.

11. Chandler, *The Raymond Chandler Papers,* 28.

12. Symons, *Bloody Murder,* 137–38.

13. Bunson, *The Complete Christie,* 208 and 299; Curry is the "discreet officer."

14. Scholes and Kellogg, *The Nature of Narrative,* 165.

15. Forster, *Aspects of the Novel,* 62.

16. Green, "Why Human Beings Are Interested in Crime," 39; italics in the original, xx.

17. Christie, "Agatha Christie on Mystery Fiction," 28."

18. Kenney, "Detecting a Novel Use," 127.

19. Bayard, *Who Killed Roger Ackroyd?* 67, italics in the original, xx. Bayard elaborates further on these points, positing the challenge of resolving the author's movements between opening and foreclosing meanings: "Now, these two movements are essentially contradictory. . . . The second movement, which proposes a unique textual truth, certainly attempts to cancel the multiple meanings organized up to this point by substituting a single meaning presented as necessary after the fact. But so many hypotheses are

generated by the combination of different possible decoys that the movement of foreclosure runs a serious risk of leaving a certain number intact" (67–68). In other words, the conclusions of some mystery novels may be more inconclusive than their authors might intend.

20. Freeman, "The Art of the Detective Story," 17.

21. Singer, "The Whodunit as Riddle," 166 and 158.

22. For Freytag's structural analysis of narrative, see his *Technique of the Drama,* 131–32.

23. While praising Dickens and Dumas, she simultaneously conceded, "I have never been able to appreciate Thackeray as I should" (*Autobiography,* 137).

24. Makinen, "Agatha Christie in Dialogue."

25. Birns and Birns, "Agatha Christie: Modern and Modernist," 123.

26. Eliot, "Little Gidding," lines 232–33, from *Four Quartets.*

27. Prescott, "Books of the Times," 19.

28. "*Indian Scene* and Other Recent Works," BR7.

29. Mary Westmacott, pseudonym of Agatha Christie, *The Burden* (1956; Dell, 1967).

30. Gill, *Agatha Christie,* 156.

SIX: The Tragicomic Themes of Christie's Murders

1. Agatha Christie, quoted in Rowse, *Memories,* 93.

2. DeMarr, "The Comic Village," 76.

3. This formulation has deep roots in the heteronormative expectation of reproduction in marriage, a narrative conclusion not (or no longer) denied to queer couples but one that requires enactment through a range of imaginative ways.

4. Thompson, *Agatha Christie,* 68.

5. Knepper, "Reading Agatha Christie's Miss Marple Series," 68.

6. Hirst, *Comedy of Manners,* 1.

7. Hirst, *Comedy of Manners,* 2.

8. McDonald, "Three Poirots on a Train," 130.

9. Eagleton, *Tragedy,* 169.

10. Langer, "The Great Dramatic Forms," 324.

11. Beran, "Love in the Absence of Judgment," 530–31.

12. Hopkins, *Shakespearean Allusion in Crime Fiction,* 10.

SEVEN: The Queer Insularity of Christie's England

1. Agatha Christie, quoted in *Time,* "Dame Agatha," 75.

2. Thompson, *Agatha Christie,* 353.

3. Moon, "Agatha Christie," 72.

4. Bernthal, *Queering Agatha Christie,* 264.

5. *Oxford English Dictionary,* s.v. "insular," 4 (a); https://www.oed.com.

6. *Oxford English Dictionary,* s.v. "pukka"; compounds, "pukka sahib."

7. Allmendinger, "The Erasure of Race," 60.

8. Freeman, *The Red Thumb Mark,* ix–x.

9. Marsh, *A Man Lay Dead,* 37.

10. James, *The Lighthouse,* 3.

11. Moon, "Agatha Christie," 70.

12. On the potential queerness of dandyism, see Janes, *Oscar Wilde Prefigured.*

13. Lucchesi, "'The Dandy in Me,'" 163.

14. Munn, *Murder by the Book?* 8.

15. Mezei, "Spinsters, Surveillance, and Speech," 104.

16. In contrast to Miss Brent's death following her cruelty to a pregnant teen, another of Christie's victims, Miss Crabtree, is murdered by the son of her maid Martha, who years ago found herself "in trouble": "I got into trouble, sir, when I was a girl, and Miss Crabtree stood by me—took me back into her service, she did, when it was all over" ("Sing a Song of Sixpence," *Witness for the Prosecution,* 133).

EIGHT: Christie's Murders at the Movies . . . and Why She Disliked Them

1. Cartmell and Whelehan, *Screen Adaptation,* 12.

2. Otto Penzler, quoted in Fryxell, "All about Agatha," 45.

3. Hesse, "Assumed Identity," 196. With these words, Hesse specifically refers to theatrical adaptations, yet her point applies equally to cinematic adaptations.

4. This brief overview of film and television adaptations of Christie's publications is indebted to Mark Aldridge's *Agatha Christie on Screen;* see also his *Agatha Christie's Poirot.*

5. Lord Snowdon, "'What do you expect of 83?'" 29.

6. Agatha Christie, quoted in Thompson, *Agatha Christie,* 432.

7. Haining, *Agatha Christie: Murder in Four Acts,* 140.

8. Aldridge, *Agatha Christie on Screen,* 287–310.

9. Macdonell, "*Alibi:* By M. Morton," 533.

10. Lord Snowdon, "'What do you expect of 83?'" 29.

11. See McCarver, *The Case of Compartment,* 7, and "Finding the Queen of Mystery."

12. Sontag, "Notes on 'Camp,'" 279.

13. Sontag, "Notes on 'Camp,'" 284.

14. Meyer, "Introduction: Reclaiming the Discourse of Camp," 11.

15. Core, *Camp: The Lie That Tells the Truth,* 9.

16. Barry Sandler, phone interview with the author, 27 January 2017.

17. Jenkinson, "The Agatha Christie Films," 177.

18. Gibbs, "The Theatre: Fair Enough," 32.

19. York, *Agatha Christie: Power and Illusion,* 41.

20. Makinen, *Agatha Christie: Investigating Femininity,* 82.

21. Dyer, "It's Being So Camp as Keeps Us Going," 13.

22. On the "aging diva phenomenon," see Flynn, "The Deaths of Camp," who cites "Elizabeth Taylor on the cover of *Hollywood Babylon II*" to illustrate this stock figure of camp (444).

23. Barry Sandler, phone interview with the author, 27 January 2017.

24. "Tea-Cozy Mischief," 20.

25. "Review of *The Mirror Crack'd*," 48.

26. "Stay Home with a Good Game of Clue," 58.

27. Reed, "Movies: *The Mirror Crack'd*," 27.

28. Thompson, "Off the Wall: *The Mirror Crack'd*," 59.

29. "Stay Home with a Good Game of Clue," 58.

30. Reed, "Movies: *The Mirror Crack'd*," 27.

31. "Tea-Cozy Mischief," 20.

32. Smith, "Communicating to the Audience." *New York Social Diary*.

33. York, *Agatha Christie: Power and Illusion*, 69.

Conclusion: Literary Criticism and the Mystery of Christie's Murderous Pleasures

1. Agatha Christie, quoted in "The Talk of the Town," 24.

2. Mallowan, *Mallowan's Memoirs*, 206.

3. Hannah, "No One Should Condescend to Agatha Christie."

4. Orwell, *Shooting an Elephant*, 186.

BIBLIOGRAPHY

Primary Sources

AGATHA CHRISTIE'S DETECTIVE FICTION

Citations from these books are taken from *The Agatha Christie Mystery Collection*, published by Bantam in the 1980s and 1990s.

The Mysterious Affair at Styles. 1920.
The Secret Adversary. 1922.
Murder on the Links. 1923.
The Man in the Brown Suit. 1924.
Poirot Investigates. 1924.
The Secret of Chimneys. 1925.
The Murder of Roger Ackroyd. 1926.
The Big Four. 1927.
The Mystery of the Blue Train. 1928.
The Seven Dials Mystery. 1929.
Partners in Crime. 1929.
The Mysterious Mr. Quin. 1930.
The Murder at the Vicarage. 1930.
The Sittaford Mystery / Murder at Hazelmoor. 1931.
Peril at End House. 1932.
The Thirteen Problems / The Tuesday Club Murders. 1932.
Lord Edgware Dies / Thirteen at Dinner. 1933.
The Hound of Death. 1933.
Murder on the Orient Express / Murder in the Calais Coach. 1934.
The Listerdale Mystery. 1934.
Why Didn't They Ask Evans? / The Boomerang Clue. 1934.
Parker Pyne Investigates / Mr. Parker Pyne, Detective. 1934.
Three Act Tragedy / Murder in Three Acts. 1934.
Death in the Clouds / Death in the Air. 1935.
The ABC Murders / The Alphabet Murders. 1936.
Murder in Mesopotamia. 1936.
Cards on the Table. 1936.
Dumb Witness / Poirot Loses a Client. 1937.

Death on the Nile. 1937.

Murder in the Mews / Dead Man's Mirror. 1937.

Appointment with Death. 1938.

Hercule Poirot's Christmas / Murder for Christmas / A Holiday for Murder. 1938.

Easy to Kill. 1939.

And Then There Were None / Ten Little Indians / Ten Little N------. 1939.

The Regatta Mystery and Other Stories. 1939.

Sad Cypress. 1940.

One, Two, Buckle My Shoe / The Patriotic Murders. 1940

Evil under the Sun. 1941.

N or M? 1941.

The Body in the Library. 1942.

Five Little Pigs / Murder in Retrospect. 1942.

The Moving Finger / The Case of the Moving Finger. 1942.

Towards Zero. 1944.

Death Comes as the End. 1945.

Sparkling Cyanide / Remembered Death. 1945

The Hollow / Murder after Hours. 1946.

The Labors of Hercules. 1947.

Taken at the Flood / There Is a Tide . . . 1948.

Witness for the Prosecution. 1948.

Crooked House. 1949.

A Murder Is Announced. 1950.

Three Blind Mice / The Mousetrap. 1950.

They Came to Baghdad. 1951.

The Under Dog and Other Stories. 1951.

Mrs. McGinty's Dead. 1952.

They Do It with Mirrors / Murder with Mirrors. 1952.

After the Funeral / Funerals Are Fatal. 1953.

A Pocket Full of Rye. 1953.

Destination Unknown / So Many Steps to Death. 1954.

Hickory Dickory Dock / Hickory Dickory Death. 1955.

Dead Man's Folly. 1956.

4.50 from Paddington / What Mrs. McGillicuddy Saw! 1957.

Ordeal by Innocence. 1958.

Cat among the Pigeons. 1959.

The Adventure of the Christmas Pudding. 1960.

The Pale Horse. 1961.

Double Sin and Other Stories. 1961.

The Mirror Crack'd from Side to Side / The Mirror Crack'd. 1962.

The Clocks. 1963.

A Caribbean Mystery. 1964.

At Bertram's Hotel. 1965.

Third Girl. 1966.

Endless Night. 1967.
By the Pricking of My Thumbs. 1968.
Hallowe'en Party. 1969.
Passenger to Frankfurt. 1970.
Nemesis. 1971.
The Golden Ball and Other Stories. 1971.
Elephants Can Remember. 1972.
Postern of Fate. 1973.
Poirot's Early Cases. 1974.
Curtain. 1975.
Sleeping Murder. 1976.

WORKS PUBLISHED UNDER THE PSEUDONYM MARY WESTMACOTT

Giant's Bread. 1930. Dell, 1964.
Unfinished Portrait. 1934. Dell, 1977.
Absent in the Spring. 1944. Bantam, 1992.
The Rose and the Yew Tree. 1948. Dell, 1964.
A Daughter's a Daughter. 1952. Dell, 1967.
The Burden. 1956. Dell, 1967.

PRODUCED AND PUBLISHED PLAYS

For a complete account of Christie's unproduced and unpublished plays, see Julius Green, *Curtain Up,* 561–66. Several of the following plays are collected in the anthology *The Mousetrap and Other Plays,* Introduction by Ira Levin (Dodd, Mead, 1978), with page number citations prefaced by *TMAOP.*

Black Coffee. Performed 1930; published 1934. Samuel French, 1961.
And Then There Were None. (Also produced as *Ten Little Indians / Ten Little N------.*) Performed 1943; published 1944. *TMAOP,* 1–72.
Hidden Horizon. (Also produced as *Murder on the Nile.*) Performed 1944; published 1948.
Appointment with Death. Performed 1945; published 1956. *TMAOP,* 73–158.
Towards Zero. Performed 1945; published 1978. *TMAOP,* 423–96.
The Hollow. (Also produced as *The Suspects.*) Performed 1951; published 1952. *TMAOP,* 159–260.
The Mousetrap. Performed 1952; published 1954. *TMAOP,* 261–336.
Witness for the Prosecution. Performed 1953; published 1954. *TMAOP,* 337–422.
Spider's Web. Performed 1954; published Samuel French, 1954.
Verdict. Performed 1953; published 1958. *TMAOP,* 497–572.
The Unexpected Guest. Performed 1958; published Samuel French, 1958.
Go Back for Murder. Performed 1960; published 1960. *TMAOP,* 573–659.
Rule of Three: The Rats, Afternoon at the Seaside, The Patient. Performed 1961; published Samuel French, 1963.
Akhnaton. Performed 1980; published Dodd Mead, 1973.

AUTOBIOGRAPHICAL AND MISCELLANEOUS WRITINGS

"Agatha Christie on Mystery Fiction." *The Writer* Aug. 1966: 27–28.

An Autobiography. 1977. Bantam, 1990.

Come, Tell Me How You Live. 1946. Bantam, 1985.

"Introduction." *The Mousetrap Man* by Peter Saunders. Collins, 1972. 7–9.

The Grand Tour: Around the World with the Queen of Mystery, edited by Mathew Prichard. HarperCollins, 2012.

Poems. Collins, 1973.

Star over Bethlehem and Other Stories. 1965. Bantam, 1996.

Secondary Sources Cited and Consulted

Acocella, Joan. "Queen of Crime." *The New Yorker,* 16 August 2010, 82ff.

Aldridge, Mark. *Agatha Christie on Screen.* London: Palgrave Macmillan, 2016.

———. *Agatha Christie's Poirot: The Greatest Detective in the World.* New York: HarperCollins, 2020.

Allmendinger, Blake. "The Erasure of Race in Agatha Christie's *And Then There Were None.*" *ANQ* 32, no. 1 (2019): 60–64.

Barnard, Robert. *A Talent to Deceive: An Appreciation of Agatha Christie.* New York: Mysterious Press, 1987.

Bayard, Pierre. *Who Killed Roger Ackroyd? The Mystery behind the Agatha Christie Mystery.* New York: New Press, 2000.

Benedict, Marie. *The Mystery of Mrs. Christie.* New York: Sourcebooks, 2021.

Beran, Ondřej. "Love in the Absence of Judgment." *Philosophy and Literature* 43, no. 2 (2019): 519–34.

Bernthal, J. C. "'If not yourself, who would you be?' Writing the Female Body in Agatha Christie's Second World War Detective Fiction." *Women: A Cultural Review* 26, no. 1–2 (2015): 40–56.

———. *Queering Agatha Christie: Revisiting the Golden Age of Detective Fiction.* London: Palgrave Macmillan, 2016.

Birns, Nicholas, and Margaret Boe Birns. "Agatha Christie: Modern and Modernist." In *The Cunning Craft: Original Essays on Detective Fiction and Contemporary Literary Theory,* edited by Ronald G. Walker and June Frazier, 120–34. Macomb: Western Illinois University Press, 1990.

———. "Detective Fiction and the Prose of Everyday Life: Agatha Christie, Margery Allingham, Ngaio Marsh, and Gladys Mitchell in the 1950s." In *The 1950s: A Decade of Modern British Fiction,* edited by Nick Bentley, Alice Ferrebe, and Nick Hubble, 205–33. London: Bloomsbury, 2019.

Bloom, Harold, ed. *Agatha Christie.* New York: Chelsea House, 2002.

"Books: Murder Market." *Time,* 28 February 1938, 67.

Bunson, Matthew. *The Complete Christie: An Agatha Christie Encyclopedia.* New York: Pocket Books, 2000.

Cain, James M. *The Butterfly.* New York: Knopf, 1947.

Carr, John Dickson. *The Hollow Man.* Miami, FL: Orion Books, 2002. (First published in 1935)

Cartmell, Deborah, and Imelda Whelehan. *Screen Adaptation: Impure Cinema.* London: Palgrave Macmillan, 2010.

Cawelti, John. *Adventure, Mystery, and Romance: Formula Stories as Art and Popular Culture.* Chicago: University of Chicago Press, 1976.

Chandler, Raymond. *The Raymond Chandler Papers: Selected Letters and Nonfiction, 1909–1959,* edited by Tom Hiney and Frank MacShane. New York: Atlantic Monthly Press, 2000.

———. "The Simple Art of Murder." In *The Art of the Mystery Story: A Collection of Critical Essays,* edited by Howard Haycraft, 222–37. New York: Biblo & Tannen, 1976.

Chesterton, G. K. "A Defence of Detective Stories." In *The Art of the Mystery Story: A Collection of Critical Essays,* edited by Howard Haycraft, 3–6. New York: Biblo & Tannen, 1976.

Cogdill, Oline. "Birth of a Cozy Writer." *Mystery Scene* 113 (2010): 22–24.

Core, Philip. *Camp: The Lie That Tells the Truth.* Los Angeles: Delilah Books, 1984.

Culhane, John. "The Woman with a Knack for Murder." *Reader's Digest,* 1 October 1985: 92ff.

Curran, John. *Agatha Christie: Murder in the Making: More Stories and Secrets from Her Notebooks.* New York: HarperCollins, 2011.

———. *Agatha Christie's Secret Notebooks: Fifty Years of Mysteries in the Making.* New York: HarperCollins, 2009.

Delamater, Jerome, and Ruth Prigozy, eds. *The Detective in American Fiction, Film, and Television.* Westport, CT: Greenwood Press, 1998.

DeMarr, Mary Jean. "The Comic Village." In *Comic Crime,* edited by Earl F. Bargainnier, 75–91. Madison, WI: Popular Press, 1987.

"The Detection Club Oath." In *The Art of the Mystery Story: A Collection of Critical Essays,* edited by Howard Haycraft, 197–99. New York: Biblo & Tannen, 1976.

Doyle, Arthur Conan. *The Complete Sherlock Holmes.* 2 vols. New York: Doubleday, 1930.

Dyer, Richard. "It's Being So Camp as Keeps Us Going." *Body Politic* 10 (1977): 11–13.

———. *Stars.* London: British Film Institute, 1979.

Eagleton, Terry. *Tragedy.* New Haven, CT: Yale University Press, 2020.

Edwards, Martin. *The Golden Age of Murder: The Mystery of the Writers Who Invented the Modern Detective Story.* New York: HarperCollins, 2015.

Eliot, T. S. *Four Quartets.* San Diego, CA: Harcourt Brace, 1943, 1971.

"The Escape of Agatha Christie." *Christianity Today,* 13 February 1976, 38.

Ewers, Chris. "Genre in Transit: Agatha Christie, Trains, and the Whodunit." *Journal of Narrative Theory* 46, no. 1 (2016): 97–120.

Faktorovich, Anna. *The Formulas of Popular Fiction: Elements of Fantasy, Science Fiction, Romance, Religious, and Mystery Novels.* Jefferson, NC: McFarland, 2014.

"15,000 Hunt Vainly for Mrs. Christie." *New York Times,* 13 December 1926, 1.

Flynn, Caryl. "The Deaths of Camp." In *Camp: Queer Aesthetics and the Performing Subject,* edited by Fabio Cleto, 433–57. Ann Arbor: University of Michigan Press, 1999.

Forster, E. M. *Aspects of the Novel.* Cambridge, UK: Harvest, 1954. (First published in 1927)

Freeman, R. Austin. "The Art of the Detective Story." In *The Art of the Mystery Story: A Collection of Critical Essays,* edited by Howard Haycraft, 7–17. New York: Biblo & Tannen, 1976.

———. *The Red Thumb Mark.* New York: Norton, 1907, 1967.

Freytag, Gustav. *Technique of the Drama: An Exposition of Dramatic Composition and Art.* 2nd ed. Translated by Elias J. MacEwan. Griggs, 1896. (Original work published 1863)

Fryxell, David. "All about Agatha." *Horizon,* November 1984, 42–45.

Gaboriau, Emile. *The Widow Lerouge.* New York: Scribner's, 1905.

Gelder, Ken. *Popular Fiction: The Logics and Practices of a Literary Field.* Milton Park, UK: Routledge, 2004.

Gibbs, Wolcott. "The Theatre: Fair Enough." *The New Yorker,* 8 July 1944, 32.

Gill, Gillian. *Agatha Christie: The Woman and Her Mysteries.* New York: Free Press, 1990.

Grant, Ellsworth. "A Tribute to Agatha Christie." *Horizon,* Autumn 1976, 106–9.

Green, Anna Katharine. *The Leavenworth Case.* London: Penguin, 2010. (First published in 1878)

———. "Why Human Beings Are Interested in Crime." *American Magazine,* February 1919: 39–40, 84–86.

Green, Julius. *Curtain Up: Agatha Christie, A Life in the Theatre.* New York: HarperCollins, 2015.

Grossvogel, David. "Agatha Christie: Containment of the Unknown." In *The Poetics of Murder,* edited by Glenn Most and William Stowe, 252–65. San Diego, CA: Harcourt Brace Jovanovich, 1983.

Haining, Peter. *Agatha Christie: Murder in Four Acts: A Centenary Celebration of "The Queen of Crime" on Stage, Film, Radio & TV.* Virgin, 1990.

Hannah, Sophie. "No One Should Condescend to Agatha Christie—She's a Genius." *The Guardian,* 16 May 2015.

Haycraft, Howard, ed. *The Art of the Mystery Story: A Collection of Critical Essays.* New York: Biblo & Tannen, 1976.

Heissenbüttel, Helmut. "Rules of the Game of the Crime Novel." In *The Poetics of Murder,* edited by Glenn Most and William Stowe, 79–92. San Diego, CA: Harcourt Brace Jovanovich, 1983.

Hesse, Beatrix. "Assumed Identity: Agatha Christie's Novels Adapted for the Stage." In *Questions of Identity in Detective Fiction,* edited by Linda Martz and Anita Higgie, 191–202. Newcastle upon Tyne, UK: Cambridge Scholars, 2007.

Hirst, David. *Comedy of Manners.* London: Methuen, 1979.

Holgate, Mike. *Stranger Than Fiction: Agatha Christie's True Crime Inspirations.* Cheltenham, UK: History Press, 2010.

Holquist, Michael. "Murder She Says." *New Republic,* 26 July 1975, 26–28.

Hopkins, Lisa. *Shakespearean Allusion in Crime Fiction: DCI Shakespeare.* London: Palgrave Macmillan, 2016.

Humble, Nicola. *The Feminine Middlebrow Novel, 1920s to 1950s: Class, Domesticity, and Bohemianism.* Oxford: Oxford University Press, 2001.

"*Indian Scene* and Other Recent Works." *New York Times,* 9 December 1934, BR7.

Irvin, Kay. "New Mystery Stories." *New York Times,* 11 September 1938, 122.

James, P. D. *The Lighthouse.* London: Faber & Faber, 2005.

———. *Talking about Detective Fiction.* New York: Knopf, 2009.

Janes, Dominic. *Oscar Wilde Prefigured: Queer Fashioning and British Caricature, 1750–1900.* Chicago: University of Chicago Press, 2016.

Jenkinson, Philip. "The Agatha Christie Films." In *Agatha Christie: First Lady of Crime,* edited by Henry Keating, 157–82. New York: Holt, 1977.

"Keeping Posted." *Saturday Evening Post,* 7 November 1935, 108.

Kenney, Catherine. "Detecting a Novel Use for Spinsters in Sayers's Fiction." In *Old Maids to Radical Spinsters: Unmarried Women in the Twentieth-Century Novel,* edited by Nina Auerbach and Laura L. Doan, 123–38. Champaign: University of Illinois Press, 1991.

Kingston, Anne. "The Ultimate Whodunit: Agatha Christie's Mysteries May Reveal Alzheimer's Clues." *Maclean's,* 6 April 2009, 45.

Knepper, Marty. "Reading Agatha Christie's Miss Marple Series: The Thirteen Problems." *Mystery Scene* 49 (September / October 1995): 16, 68–77.

Knight, Stephen. *Secrets of Crime Fiction Classics: Detecting the Delights of 21 Enduring Stories.* Jefferson, NC: McFarland, 2015.

Knox, Ronald A. "A Detective Story Decalogue." In *The Art of the Mystery Story: A Collection of Critical Essays,* edited by Howard Haycraft, 194–96. New York: Biblo & Tannen, 1976.

Langer, Susanne. "The Great Dramatic Forms: The Tragic Rhythm." In *Tragedy,* edited by John Drakakis and Naomi Conn Liebler, 323–36. London: Longman, 1998.

Lecercle, Jean-Jacques. "Three Accounts of Literary Style." *CR: The New Centennial Review* 16, no. 3 (2016): 151–72.

Leitch, Thomas. "Wanted: A New Theory of the Cozy." *Mystery Scene* 65 (1999): 77–78.

Lucchesi, Joe. "'The Dandy in Me': Romaine Brooks's 1923 Portraits." In *Dandies: Fashion and Finesse in Art and Culture,* edited by Susan Fillin-Yeh, 153–84. New York: New York University Press, 2001.

Macdonell, A. G. "*Alibi.* By M. Morton." *The London Mercury,* September 1928: 531–33.

Madden, David. "Anne Riordan: Raymond Chandler's Forgotten Heroine." In *The Detective in American Fiction, Film, and Television,* edited by Jerome Delamater and Ruth Prigozy, 3–11. Westport, CT: Greenwood Press, 1998.

Makinen, Merja. *Agatha Christie: Investigating Femininity.* London: Palgrave Macmillan, 2006.

———. "Agatha Christie in Dialogue with *To the Lighthouse:* The Modernist Artist." In *The Ageless Agatha Christie: Essays on the Mysteries and the Legacy,* edited by J. C. Bernthal, 11–28. Jefferson, NC: McFarland, 2016.

———. "Contradicting the Golden Age: Reading Agatha Christie in the Twenty-First Century." In *Criminal Moves: Modes of Mobility in Crime Fiction,* edited by Jesper

Gulddal, Alistair Rolls, and Stewart King, 77–92. Liverpool, UK: Liverpool University Press, 2019.

Mallowan, Max. *Mallowan's Memoirs: The Autobiography of Max Mallowan.* Cork, Ireland: Collins, 1977.

"The Mallowans." *New Yorker,* 29 October 1966, 51–52.

Marsh, Ngaio. *A Man Lay Dead.* New York: Felony & Mayhem, 2011. (First published in 1934)

McCarver, Sam. *The Case of Compartment 7.* London: Penguin Putnam, 2000.

———. "Finding the Queen of Mystery." *The Writer,* October 2005, 43–44.

McDonald, Neil. "Three Poirots on a Train." *Quadrant,* January–February 2018, 129–31.

Meyer, Moe. "Introduction: Reclaiming the Discourse of Camp." In *The Politics and Poetics of Camp,* edited by Moe Meyer, 1–22. Milton Park, UK: Routledge, 1994.

Mezei, Kathy. "Spinsters, Surveillance, and Speech: The Case of Miss Marple, Miss Mole, and Miss Jekyll." *Journal of Modern Literature* 30, no. 2 (2007): 103–20.

"Mistress of Mystery." *Newsweek,* 26 January 1976, 69.

"Mme. Whodunit." *Good Housekeeping,* March 1958, 13.

Mochrie, Margaret. "They Make Crime Pay." *The Delineator,* February 1937, 28ff.

Moon, Michael. "Agatha Christie: Norms and Codes." In *Murder in the Closet: Essays on Queer Clues in Crime Fiction before Stonewall,* edited by Curtis Evans, 67–77. Jefferson, NC: McFarland, 2016.

Most, Glenn, and William Stowe, eds. *The Poetics of Murder.* San Diego, CA: Harcourt Brace Jovanovich, 1983.

"Mrs. Christie Has Lost Memory." *New York Times,* 17 December 1926, 4.

Mundow, Anna. "*Agatha Christie* Review: The Queen of the Cozy." *Wall Street Journal,* 3 March 2018, C5.

Munn, Sally R. *Murder by the Book? Feminism and the Crime Novel.* Milton Park, UK: Routledge, 1994.

Neimark, Paul. "Human Nature Is the Culprit: *Endless Night.*" *New York Times,* 17 May 1968, BR49.

"New Mystery Stories." *New York Times,* 16 February 1936, BR25.

Norman, Andrew. *Agatha Christie: The Finished Portrait.* Gloucestershire, UK: Tempus, 2006.

O'Brien, Geoffrey. *Hardboiled America: Lurid Paperbacks and the Masters of Noir.* Boston: Da Capo Press, 1997.

Orwell, George. *Shooting an Elephant and Other Essays.* San Diego, CA: Harcourt Brace Jovanovich, 1945.

Palmer, Scott. *The Films of Agatha Christie.* London: Batsford, 1993.

Petschek, Willa. "Agatha Christie: The World's Most Mysterious Woman." *McCall's,* February 1969, 8off.

Plain, Gill. "'Tale Engineering': Agatha Christie and the Aftermath of the Second World War." *Literature & History* 29, no. 2 (2020): 179–99.

Poe, Edgar Allan. *The Collected Tales and Poems of Edgar Allan Poe.* New York: Modern Library, 1992.

Powers, Anne. *True Crime Parallels to the Mysteries of Agatha Christie.* Jefferson, NC: McFarland, 2020.

Prescott, Orville. "Books of the Times." *The New York Times,* 27 September 1944, 19.

Queen, Ellery. *The Siamese Twin Mystery.* Philadelphia: Blakiston, 1933.

Redmond, Sean. *Celebrity.* Milton Park, UK: Routledge, 2018.

Reed, Rex. "Movies: *The Mirror Crack'd.*" *Vogue,* January 1981, 27.

"Review of *The Mirror Crack'd.*" *New York,* 29 December 1980–5 January 1981, 48.

Rowland, Susan. "Cooking the Books: Metafictional Myth and Ecocritical Magic in 'Cozy' Mysteries from Agatha Christie to Contemporary Cooking Sleuths." In *New Perspectives on Detective Fiction: Mystery Magnified,* edited by Casey Cothran and Mercy Cannon, 157–72. Milton Park, UK: Routledge, 2016.

Rowse, A. L. *Memories of Men and Women, American and British.* Lanham, MD: University Press of America, 1984.

Sandbrook Dominic. "Clever-clogs Critics Who Sneer at Agatha Christie Make Me Murderous: Dominic Sandbrook Explains Why Author's Thrillers Are Always Worth a Read." *Daily Mail,* 28 December 2015.

Sandler, Barry. Phone interview with the author, 27 January 2017.

———, screenwriter. *The Mirror Crack'd.* Dir. Guy Hamilton. Screenplay co-credited to Jonathan Hales. Perf. Elizabeth Taylor, Rock Hudson, and Angela Lansbury. 1980. Lions Gate, 2009.

Scholes, Robert, and Robert Kellogg. *The Nature of Narrative.* Oxford: Oxford University Press, 1966.

Shenker, Israel. "The Past Master of Mysteries, She Built a Better Mousetrap." *Smithsonian,* September 1990, 86ff.

Singer, Eliot. "The Whodunit as Riddle: Block Elements in Agatha Christie." *Western Folklore* 43, no. 3 (1984): 157–71.

Smith, Liz. "Communicating to the Audience." *New York Social Diary,* 12 February 2015.

Snowdon, Lord. "'What do you expect of 83 if you can't have a rest from writing?' Agatha Christie Interviewed by Lord Snowdon." *Australian Women's Weekly,* 18 September 1974, 29ff.

Sontag, Susan. "Notes on 'Camp.'" In *Against Interpretation and Other Essays,* 275–92. Norwell, MA: Anchor, 1986.

Spenser, Edmund. *The Faerie Queen.* New York: Penguin, 1978.

Stasio, Marilyn. "Murder Least Foul: The Cozy, Soft-Boiled Mystery." *New York Times,* 18 October 1992, BR42–43.

"Stay Home with a Good Game of Clue: *The Mirror Crack'd.*" *Maclean's,* 22 December 1980, 58.

Stern, Philip Van Doren. "The Case of the Corpse in the Blind Alley." *Virginia Quarterly* 17, no. 2 (1941): 227–36.

Strachey, John. "The Golden Age of English Detection." *Saturday Review of Literature,* 7 January 1939, 12–14.

Symons, Julian. *Bloody Murder: From the Detective Story to the Crime Novel.* 3rd ed. New York: Mysterious Press, 1992.

"The Talk of the Town." *New Yorker*, 26 January 1976, 23–27.

"Tea-Cozy Mischief." *Newsweek*, 19 January 1981, 20.

Thompson, Laura. *Agatha Christie: A Mysterious Life*. New York: Pegasus Books, 2018.

———. "Dame Agatha: Queen of the Maze." *Time*, 26 January 1976, 75.

———. "Off the Wall: *The Mirror Crack'd*." *Time*, 29 December 1980, 59.

Trewin, J. C. "Mixed Weather." *Illustrated London News*, 22 September 1956, 482.

Tyler, Ralph. "Curtains for Poirot." *Saturday Review*, 4 October 1975, 24–27.

Tynan, Kathleen. *Agatha*. New York: Ballantine, 1978.

Updike, John. "Agatha Christie and Beatrix Potter." *The New Yorker*, 26 November 1960, 52.

Van Dine, S. S. "S. S. Van Dine Sets Down Twenty Rules for Detective Stories." *The American Magazine*, September 1928, 129–31.

Wilson, Edmund. *Classics and Commercials: A Literary Chronicle of the Forties*. New York: Farrar, Straus, 1950.

Wren, Lassiter, and Randle McKay. *The Baffle Book*. New York: Doubleday, Doran, 1928.

Yang, Amy. "Psychoanalysis and Detective Fiction: A Tale of Freud and Criminal Storytelling." *Perspectives in Biology and Medicine* 53, no. 4 (2010): 596–604.

Yiannitsaros, Christopher. "'Tea and scandal at four-thirty': Fantasies of Englishness and Agatha Christie's Fiction of the 1930s and 1940s." *Clues: A Journal of Detection* 35, no. 2 (2017): 78–88.

York, R. A. *Agatha Christie: Power and Illusion*. London: Palgrave Macmillan, 2007.